Sew Your Own

Fashion
Accessories

Sew Your Own

Fashion Accessories

Rusty Bensussen

Sterling Publishing Co., Inc.   New York

Library of Congress Cataloging-in-Publication Data

Bensussen, Rusty.
    Sew your own fashion accessories / written and illustrated by
Rusty Bensussen.
        p.   cm.
    ISBN 0-8069-5745-X
    1. Dress accessories.   I. Title.
TT560.B37   1990
646.4'8—dc20
                                                                89-49404
                                                                    CIP

Copyright © 1990 by Estelle Bensussen
Published by Sterling Publishing Co., Inc.
387 Park Avenue South, New York, N.Y. 10016
Distributed in Canada by Oak Tree Press Ltd.
℅ Canadian Manda Group, P.O. Box 920, Station U
Toronto, Ontario, Canada M8Z 5P9
Distributed in Great Britain and Europe by Cassell PLC
Artillery House, Artillery Row, London SW1P 1RT, England
Distributed in Australia by Capricorn Ltd.
P.O. Box 665, Lane Cove, NSW 2066
Manufactured in the United States of America
All rights reserved

BOMC offers recordings and compact discs, cassettes
and records. For information and catalog write to
BOMR, Camp Hill, PA 17012.

CONTENTS

Acknowledgments 7

Introduction 9

What Is a Wardrobe? • What's in Your Closet? • Turn Your World Around • Found Fabric • Seasonal Wardrobes • About This Book

Color a Personal Rainbow 16

Blonde • Redhead • Brunette

Dickeys 29

The Basic Dickey • Basic Dickey Pattern from Measurements • Cuffs • Ruffled Dickey • Dickey with Pleated Neckband • Pleated Dickey • Dickeys from Knitted Fabric • Transformation Dickey

Scarves 46

Padded Head Scarf • Turban • Fishnet Triangle • Lettuce Edge Ruffled Jabot • Ascot • Theatre Scarf • Aviator's Scarf

Belts 75

Ultrasuede Belts • Assorted Belts with Buckles • Double-Wrapped Belts • Embroidered Belts • Rope Belts • Cabbage Rose Belt

Flounces, Peplums, and Overskirts 90

Peplum: Straight Cut • Peplum: Circle Cut • Peplum: Asymmetric Hemline • Peplum: Circular Asymmetric • Tiered Overskirts • Flamenco-Style Overskirt • Pocket Peplum

Hats and Other Head Coverings 111

Beret • Unlined Beret • Reversible Beret • Darted Beret • Beret with Brim • Pie-Slice Large Beret • Ribbon Beret • Cocktail Hats • Cabbage Rose Hat • Variation on the Visor • Ribbons and Bows

Fabric Flowers and Leaves 124

Cabbage Rose • Small Roses • Lazy Daisies • Leaf Collar

Decorations That Glitter 134

Quilted Jewelry 138

Epilogue: Fashion and Fancy 147

Metric Equivalency Chart 151

Index 152

About the Author 155

ACKNOWLEDGMENTS

My thanks to Caryl Weldon, color consultant, for the use of her expertise; Barbara Busch, editor, for her extra efforts on my behalf; and Charlie, because he's Charlie.

Illus. 1.

INTRODUCTION

According to Webster, a wardrobe is a person's collection of usable clothing for one or more seasons (Illus. 1). But don't let this very simple definition fool you! Usable clothing doesn't become a wardrobe until you add a workable selection of quality accessories that extend the use of the basic garments, puts your personal stamp on assembled clothing and expands the scope of each outfit.

Accessories are the link between wardrobe standbys and new purchases (Illus. 2). They bridge the gap between unrelated separates and coordinated costumes, wearable clothing and hanger-occupiers. Accessories diversify single-use garments and create an atmosphere for all-occasion dressing. They smooth out any conflict between the clothing that is within the area of your personal color needs and garments of unworkable colors that you love and can't bear to give away.

Making color work for you is not the complicated process it's made out to be. The secret, if there is one, lies in identifying your genetic colors, the colors within your skin tones, eyes and hair. They are the colors you'll use to plan the perfect wardrobe, pull everything together, and make your clothing a more personal expression.

Before you stir up your closet or start to sew the wonderful accessories in this book, read the chapter on Personal Color Planning and complete the entire survey. If you already feel good about yourself, color-planning will make you feel even better. Additional knowledge of your personal color needs will reinforce the direction you've already taken and help expand your ideas.

Illus. 2.

If you're not quite sure about the whole thing, personal color information can give you a handle on looking better than ever. It provides the solid base you need to make individual color decisions that work *for* you instead of against your natural scheme. Color-planning will turn assorted (but unrelated) separates into a working wardrobe.

What Is a Wardrobe?

A wardrobe is a personal statement that expresses how you feel about yourself, how you see yourself, and how you want the world to see you. With positive planning, your wardrobe is an exclusive, individualized statement; without positive planning, it can easily miss the mark.

A practical number of basic, well-coordinated quality garments that will hold up through repeated wear and care is your prime need. Choose only the pieces that are personally pleasing and in your most complimentary colors. Be sure these items are fash-ionable by *your* standards, not in the judgment of a well-meaning but unknowledgeable friend, or from the gleanings of an impersonal fashion article written in very general terms. Know that what's in your closet is in keeping with *your* daily activities and lifestyle. All of these choices can only be made by you; you're the only one with the answers.

Achieve a comfort zone of color, fit and reliability with your basic clothing. Add an assortment of well-chosen accessories to the collection and extend the use of each simple item. Assemble all of the above to your satisfaction and you are in possession of a versatile, wearable wardrobe (Illus. 3).

Illus. 3.

What's in Your Closet?

If you are one of the vast majority, what is currently hanging in your closet probably isn't a workable wardrobe. What your clothing collection might consist of is:

1. A group of garments in need of repair,

2. A collection of things purchased because they were on sale and you couldn't pass up a bargain (even though these bargains did not necessarily suit you, your personal color scheme or your lifestyle) and,

3. An assortment of oddments you "couldn't live without" because you were going on another diet and you just knew you'd be able to fit into these treasures in a week or two. (All garments in this group are still displaying the original tags and have never been worn.)

In addition to the aforementioned unwearable basics there may be a little group of items that you bought and only wore once. Why you decided you didn't like these garments is not the issue; what you must deal with is that these clothes are still new, still hanging in your closet, still collecting dust and will probably never again adorn your body. You keep them because it makes you feel good to have all those hangers filled. This group of clothing might even have some companions: The gems of wonderful style (wrong color) and the designer-type garments that were perfect on your 5' 11'' tall neighbor (you are only 5' 1''), in short, more hanger-clothing.

4. Somewhere, crushed between all these wonders is a very limited number of perfect standbys that you reach for when you want something special, something that fits properly, and something that always feels right.

Sure, it's fun to open your closet door and see a collection of clothing that rivals the fashion floor at your favorite department store. It's great to own a collection of wearable clothing with endless choices, a multitude of combinations, something for every given hour of the day or night. But don't overlook the key words in the above statement: *wearable clothing.* That means properly fitted clothing suited to *your* figure, *your* personal color scheme, and *your* lifestyle. It leaves no room for any of the unusables, unwearables or unworkables previously mentioned.

Trying to make a satisfactory wardrobe out of what's hanging in your closet by adding to the confusion is not going to solve the problem, either (Illus. 4). What to wear, how to

Illus. 4.

11

wear it, and where to put everything when it's not being worn can be overwhelming at best. On top of that, there's no one (except you) who can handle your clothing decisions; no one but you can bring order to your personal fashion chaos; and no one but you can supply the personal knowledge to make it all work.

There are two basic approaches to a workable wardrobe:

1. *Buy* and/or sew tons of clothing of every description to be sure you have something to wear for any occasion that might arise, or,

2. *Plan* a small but versatile wardrobe that will accommodate the lines of your figure, your personal color scheme, the needs of your activities, and the demands of your lifestyle.

Obviously, the first suggestion (buy or sew everything you see or dream up) is out of the question. Impulse, whether in sewing or buying hasn't ever been successful for anyone and it isn't going to get any better. Acquire clothing willy-nilly and you only create more problems in your already chaotic fashion world. Random purchases or unplanned sewing have a tendency to crowd you out of your house and cause expenses which can be hard to handle. Give in to shopping urges too easily and you end up with hordes of unrelated garments, jammed closets, overflowing drawers and clothing ˌ wn about every room, and, chances are tˌat you still won't have anything to wear.

The second suggestion (plan a wardrobe) is, by far, the best solution. A planned wardrobe hangs neatly in the closet; all garments highly visible, all comfortable choices, everything well coordinated and usable at a second's notice, all ready to wear and ready to pack when it's time to travel.

Turn Your World Around

How do you arrive at a workable wardrobe? With a critical assessment of the garments already in your closet, elimination of closet clutter and the determination to toss away every bit of excess baggage.

Form a practical plan for the things you deem usable and wearable. Make sensible, timely additions to plump up the bare bones, and be stubborn enough to stick with your plan. Gather all the courage you can muster and start harvesting the treasures lost at the back of your closet.

1. Eliminate the clothing you will never wear again. There are many service organizations that appreciate your donations and you will surely enjoy reclaiming some valuable closet space.

2. Set aside all items that are obviously in need of repair. Carefully survey each item (old favorites as well as seldom-worn garments) for missing buttons, broken zippers or torn seams. Make repairs to garments that will still give service and satisfaction.

3. Separate suits and other "bought together" outfits by category. Hang similar garments in separate portions of the closet: jackets with jackets, pants with pants, skirts with skirts, tops with tops. This will eliminate the feeling that matched clothing must be worn only as it comes from the store. Make room in your world for eclectic dressing.

4. When you have weeded out all the questionable items and organized the clothing you know you still want to wear, do an inventory of the things that remain. Decide whether there is enough clothing for your wants without there being too much for your lifestyle. Be

clinical about this phase. For example, you don't really need five or six formal gowns if you only go to black-tie parties once every three or four years, and you don't need six jogging suits if you only exercise once a week.

5. Experiment with the garments that remain in your closet. Try some new combinations: choice oddments with wardrobe staples, suit parts with separates. Get a fresh slant on the capabilities of what you already have. Work only with the existing garments, all suitable to you and your lifestyle. Become familiar with the possibilities and combinations of the things that are available. A change in the way you wear your clothing brings new life to old favorites. A thorough overview of what exists in your closet points up new avenues for clothing use.

6. While you experiment with these new combinations, dispose of any additional items that don't fit into your scheme. Determine what, if anything, is missing from your selection. Consider possible additions you might include after you are more familiar with the combinations on hand. If you do find that you need some additional garments, decide whether they are immediate needs or can be made part of a long-range plan.

Plot a sensible course for adding garments in the immediate category as well as long-range additions. Keep everything under control or you'll overfill that nice space in your closet before you really get to enjoy it.

7. Make sure the entire schedule for clothing additions is within your income *and* your available sewing time. Don't make outlandish plans that involve six hours of sewing every day when you work a forty-hour week. Be as practical in your allocation of time as you are with money.

Actual clothing needs vary with the individual. In today's busy world where dry-cleaning might take days instead of a few hours and laundry facilities aren't always available when you are, a basic wardrobe should include enough clothing to see you through a week of normal activities without last-minute panic-additions. Include a sensible number of skirts, pants, jackets, blouses and sweaters to adequately clothe you, day and night.

When your basic wardrobe is set up, carefully scan your clothing for versatility. Decide on accessory additions in the order of their importance. For example:

- Long scarves in several colors perk up a suit, tone basic clothing in new directions, turn a loose sheath into a fitted dress. Scarves of any type fill a daily need as well as being part of special-occasion dressing.

- Dickeys change the neckline of a blouse or sweater; bring skirt or pants color closer to the face.

- An overskirt will change the entire look of a simple dress; even eliminate the need to shop for that party you'll attend next week. If you're sitting with an invitation—and nothing to wear—this might be a starting place for you.

Found Fabric

Go through your scrap bags and reclaim pieces of fabric that match the garments you will continue to wear. Those leftover pieces of material can be used for many of the accessories detailed in this book such as: ''Fabric Flowers,'' ''Dickeys,'' or ''Quilted Jewelry.'' These are the little extras that make multi-use garments out of the basics you'll continue to wear.

Seasonal Wardrobes

If you live in an area with extreme weather changes, you probably have a separate wardrobe for each season. You will have to go through the whole process of wardrobe-gleaning with next season's clothing, but don't let it throw you. You've already done it once; you've learned how to handle the task. When it's time to weed out next season's wardrobe, follow the technique you've already used; the job will be much easier than it was the first time. You're all prepared.

About This Book

A limited number of garments are used in the illustrations to show how simple wardrobing is with the proper accessories. Limiting the clothing in the drawings demonstrates graphically how easy it is to confine your own wardrobe for the greatest wearability.

Accessories are pictured with a jewel-neck top, a V-neck top, an A-line skirt, and a straight skirt (Illus. 5). There are also some pants scattered through various chapters to present a different slant on trouser-dressing.

You will find complete cutting charts, directions and finishing information for all of the accessories shown, plus lots of ideas on extending the use of each concept. Instructions for sewing basic clothing are not included; there are other books to deal with that subject.

There are so many ideas to try, so many new and interesting things to make, a range of options from simple add-ons to glamorous

Illus. 5.

transformations. If you have difficulty deciding where to begin sewing your accessory wardrobe and which items will give you the best and most immediate results, answer the following questions. It will help you choose the starting point most important to your personal wardrobe.

1.   Which accessories are most complementary to the clothing styles you normally choose?

2.   Which accessories will be the most comfortable for you? Which are the ones you're most likely to wear?

3.   Which accessories are the most flattering to your figure?

4.   Which accessories best suit your daily activities? Your business schedule? Your social schedule? Your general lifestyle?

What you've no doubt learned from the survey is that you don't have to make every item in this book to enhance your wardrobe. However, some of the things might work for you. Be selective. First sew the accessories that will be of immediate value to your own lifestyle, things you will use every day, or at least often enough to make it worthwhile creating them. Each addition you choose for yourself should be something you'll really enjoy wearing; something to make you feel good about yourself.

Keep the untried ideas in mind for a future time. An invitation to a special event might inspire you to sew something that is not necessarily a part of your everyday costuming, such as an elaborate overskirt, a fancy cocktail hat or an extensively jewelled ornament. The items you reject for your current use are still usable ideas for special occasion accessories, gifting, or incorporating with your own ideas. Each piece you sew is a forever item. Fashion changes faster than the seasons, but handmade accessories are the treasured items that continue to personalize a wardrobe year after year.

COLOR A PERSONAL RAINBOW

The wrong choice of color has been known to turn sewing results from success to disaster in that proverbial "wink of an eye." A garment that was planned to be fantastic might end up in the giveaway box without ever having been worn. Accessories styled to coordinate the colors of some unrelated separates result in a horrible clash instead of the beautiful blend you were seeking. Mistakes of this sort are not only costly, they sap your confidence.

The ability to sew puts you in the unique position of being your own designer as well as color coordinator. You have the opportunity to make clothing in the right choice of color and style to complement *your* figure and personal color scheme. All you need to accomplish this is the confidence that grows from deep personal knowledge.

There's no need to make your color choices through guesswork. Invest a bit of time to really learn about yourself and your built-in color scheme; you will find that it's time well spent. The right colors can make a big difference in your life. They influence your attitude towards everything around you, including how you feel about yourself. Become familiar with your personal scheme of things, and you will be in command of your own wardrobe planning. *You* hold the key to your best personal color selections and are the only one who can put it all together.

Personal color analysis is an in-depth evaluation of hair, eyes, and skin, the three areas that reveal the entire scope of your color scheme (Illus. 6). Don't skim over any part of it. List all the personal color information that you can find. If you have ever had a color-

choice failure, this survey can tell you why and help you prevent it from happening again.

FINDING YOUR COLORS

You've looked at yourself for years but have you ever really *seen* yourself? "Seeing" one's own coloring isn't the easiest thing to do. If you have any doubts about your ability to do an in-depth personal color evaluation on your own, get together with a good friend and survey each other. She had better be a *good* friend as you both will have to clean away the last vestiges of any and all make-up and bare your faces as you may not have done in years. To complete your survey you will need:

- **Natural Daylight:** This is very important to a color study. Artificial light influences the results; natural light (preferably a northern exposure) shows the purest and maximum color. An uncurtained window or a window with the drapes pulled back as far as possible is your best light source.

- **A Card Table and Two Chairs** gives you a comfortable place to sit and work, with enough space to spread out your color samples.

- A **Hand-held Mirror** is needed so that you can look at yourself at the same time your friend surveys your coloring.

- **A White Shampoo Cape** or a sheet to completely cover the clothing. This will prevent the colors around you from influencing the results of the analysis.

Color Samples. Collect a basket of accessories, household items, fruit, fabric remnants, or any solid-colored item that will serve as a color swatch to hold up to your face. Visit your local paint store and select swatches from the color samples that are available. Paint chips are not only useful during the evaluation sessions but later on during shopping trips, for matching colors. Any and all of these items will graphically illustrate how different colors affect your complexion and general appearance.

LOOK INTO YOUR OWN EYES

Start your personal color evaluation with your eyes. They reveal the clearest and most obvious of your genetic colors. List the basic color of your eyes and don't overlook the colors of all the tiny flecks that appear in the iris. These colors are very important to your chart; they are your prime colors, the most complimentary to your skin tones.

Note the shade of white in the surrounding area, is it underscored with warm tones or cool ones? This tone will lead you to your best shade of white.

Illus. 6.

STUDY YOUR HAIR

Your hair yields the next group of colors and tones (Illus. 7). Try to give yourself a complete list of hair colors. Hair is not just yellow, brown or red. Search out all of those highlights and undertones; they're important. If you tint or dye your hair you will have to do a little memory-searching to come up with the original coloration but at least make an educated guess.

Have your friend check the tones of the underneath hair at the back of your head. Are those tones warm or cool? Beige-blond, strawberry or auburn lights? Golden or ashen?

Are you starting to turn grey? If so, are the grey tones towards the yellow or white shades? Prior to greying, hair often turns dark. Are these tones blue, brown or some other color? List each color as you or your companion see it.

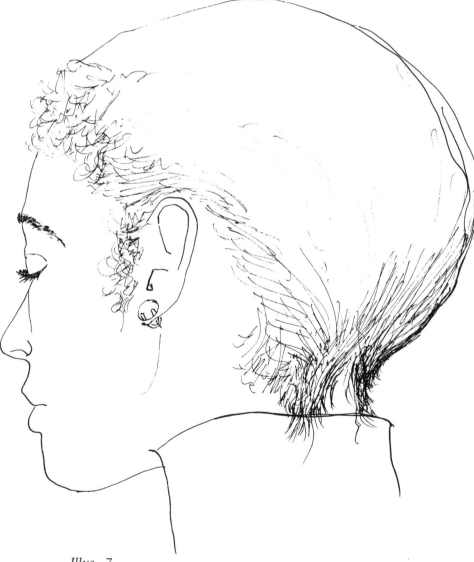

Illus. 7.

Black and Asian skin, hair and eyes are definitely included in the categories that follow. Asians will find most of their personal information under the heading of Dark Brunette.

Black women will find personal answers under several different categories. Your hair and skin tones can fall into any of the groupings: Blonde, Brunette, or Redhead. Black women, like Caucasians, are often natural blondes or redheads, not just dark brunettes. "Black" skin tones range from fair to dark, warm to cool. Study yourself carefully to find the maximum color answers.

DON'T OVERLOOK YOUR SKIN

Older skin is probably the most difficult to survey. Years of wearing make-up may have muted the natural colors of your skin tones. Scan the inside flesh of your arms while your friend checks the back of your neck and under your jawline. Each of these areas reveal colors that might not be visible on your face. Do compare your skin tones to those of others in your household as well as the person working with you. These comparisons can start you "seeing" color where you previously thought none existed. Are your skin tones pink, beige or mauve? Freckled or clear? Does your skin appear to be translucent or opaque? Each of these factors will bear on the colors and intensity that will best suit you.

When you have a good understanding of what you're looking for: your nature-given color scheme, read on. Scan all information pertaining to each hair-color category even if your coloring is not specifically part of that group. Hair and skin colors can overlap from one color category to another. For example, as a brownette you might have strands of auburn and blonde in your hair. This could bring secondary colors from the Blonde or Redhead categories into your color plan since both of these categories overlap yours. Don't be afraid to borrow from the color suggestions contained in overlapping categories. A considerable amount of information for these other color plans could also work for you.

The contrast between hair and skin will usually dictate the intensity and depth of color most flattering to you. It will also indicate whether you need clear or muted colors, pastels or strong primaries. A simple rule of thumb is:

The stronger the contrast between hair and skin, the stronger the clothing color contrasts; the weaker the personal color contrasts, the more monochromatic the clothing color scheme.

By way of examples: A person with blue-black hair and a very fair complexion will glow with color combinations such as black, stark white and a splash of bright, clear red—strong primary colors. A person with fair hair and pale skin is more likely to blossom against toned-down, paler colors, such as pastels and greyed tones; colors with less contrast: grey rather than black, taupe rather than dark brown, middle blue rather than deep navy.

Color should enhance your skin and make you look beautiful. It should not drain the natural tones of your face. If you think a color might possibly work if you wore more make-up, you're choosing the wrong color. A color held next to bare skin should compliment that skin immediately.

Now read on and have fun experimenting with your assorted collection of color samples.

Blonde (Illus. 8–13)

Blondes come in a wide variety of shades from pale, ashen blonde to brownette. This includes varieties of platinum, Nordic blonde, golden girls like the "California Blonde," and everything in between. Light brunettes with strong golden highlights are also included in this category. "Decided" blondes should first refer to the category for their original hair coloring as this will influence color choices before the new or chosen hair color.

Pay particular attention to the color of your eyes. Through color you can enhance them and make them appear large enough to walk through. The best way to do that is to use your eye colors for the garment or accessory nearest your face. This little trick makes the eyes sparkle and stand out. It enhances the blues and deepens green.

PALE BLONDES

Hair: Ashen, platinum, dark blonde, brownette (formerly blond, now brown). Usually light blonde to towhead as a child. This hair ages beautifully, turning pearly white or blue-grey.

Eyes: Blue, grey, hazel, blue/green.

Complexion: Translucent, pale, blush. Pinkish skin with some blue undertone. Your arms may show a sallow color but your cheeks will be pink.

Best Colors: Soft pinks and lavenders to plum. Light blue, ice-green, pale yellow, camel, taupe, and off-white. In other words, almost the entire range of pastels.

Avoid: Stark whites, deep yellows or orange, olive green.

If your hair has darkened over the years and leans towards the brownette or brunette shades and your skin is still rather pale, try burgundy and strong pinks, grey with a heavy

Yellow

Red

Blue

Orange

Purple

Green

Illus. 8.

Illus. 9.

Illus. 10.

20

hint of blue. With a rosier complexion you should look good in pinky reds, blue reds, full-bodied camel, taupe and purple.

DEEP BLONDES

Hair: Golden blonde, Nordic blonde, golden-brown, strawberry blonde. Your hair will probably grey to the yellowish tones. Consider coloring it to a more flattering shade as you age.

Eyes: Strong blue, green, golden brown or any combination of these colors. Usually clear color.

Complexion: Peach or ivory with golden undertones. Sometimes freckled. Strong tendency to blush.

Best Colors: You will do best in clear colors. Bright, strong blue such as a pure cerulean, golden strong yellows, coral, cream, ivory, peach, camel, tan and soft browns.

Avoid: Use stark whites only in small amounts. Charcoal grey, black, fuchsia, burgundy and other blue-reds are too heavy.

Choose small patterns and lightly textured fabrics. You can handle strong contrasts such as dark brown and off-white. With your coloring, you should be able to borrow from both sides of your color range: brownette and redhead. Look over these other suggestions and see what you can incorporate into your own wardrobe.

Pink

Brown

Olive

Beige

White

Black

Illus. 11.

Illus. 12.

Illus. 13.

21

Redhead (Illus. 14–19)

Hair: Golden copper, pure carrot-top, auburn, brown with strong red highlights.

Eyes: Blue, green, brown or any combination. Usually flecked with topaz.

Complexion: Fair, blushed or copper-toned. Golden undertones, not blue. Black skin will often lean towards this skintone.

Best Colors: Muted colors were created for you. Rich greens, strong orange, lush olive and terra cotta. Cinnamon, salmon, brick red and any of the many colors that appear in the iris of your eye.

Avoid: Stark whites, black, charcoal and other shades of grey that are toned with blue.

Although pinks, plum, burgundy and black are not your best colors, try them against your face to see how your skin will react. Color can do startling things at times. Your strongest as-

Yellow

Red

Blue

Orange

Purple

Green

Illus. 14.   *Illus. 15.*   *Illus. 16.*

set is the color of your hair; treat it like a precious jewel, showcase it, enhance it, and use that color in your clothing. There aren't *that* many natural redheads in the world, so try to make the most of what you've been given.

If you have chosen to be a redhead, you should pay careful attention to the information given for your natural hair coloration, too. Your natural coloring will influence your new color range.

Golden redheads look best in soft shades of beige, tan, salmon, olive or moss greens.

Copper-toned redheads do extremely well in pumpkin, cinnamon-brown, brick, copper, topaz and bronze. Middle blues of full-bodied color and emerald to olive green are also complimentary. Watch those muted tones. When they are *too* muted they can grey your skin and dull your hair.

Light redheads toned between carrot and strawberry will often find that the color scheme primarily designed for the golden blonde will be most effective. Cream, ecru and ivory are far better choices than pure white.

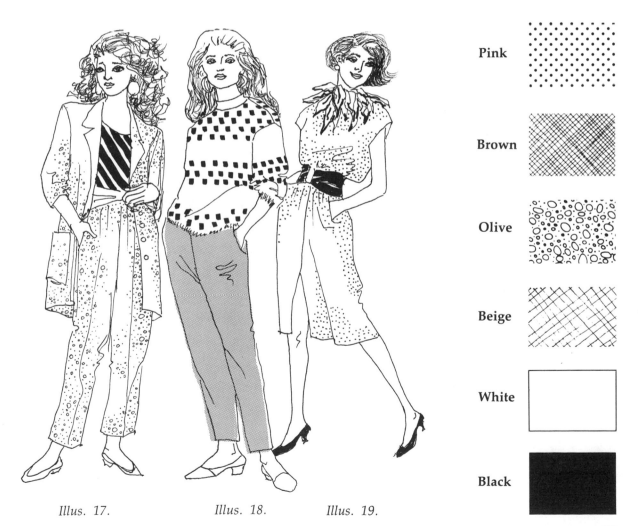

Illus. 17.   Illus. 18.   Illus. 19.

Pink

Brown

Olive

Beige

White

Black

Brunette (Illus. 20–25)

Hair: Medium to dark brown, black, jet black. This hair category tends to grey prematurely but beautifully to a salt-and-pepper or lovely silver-grey.

Eyes: Usually deep colored. Brown, hazel, dark blue, green or any combination.

Complexion: Subtle blue or blue-pink undertones. Definitely leaning towards cool colors: taupey beige, as with some Oriental and Black skin. Usually will not show rosy cheeks.

Best Colors: Red, white, black and blue; all clear, strong colors. Try those with blue undertones such as burgundy and magenta, or icy pinks, green and strong, cold yellows.

Avoid: Warm colors that are based on tones of yellow-gold or orange. Soft pastels will do nothing to enhance your vibrant color. Include muted colors with this list. They'll dull your hair and skin tones.

Olive-toned complexions need white, mauve and magenta to help them sparkle.

Fair-skinned brunettes do well in emerald green, purple and bright, true red. Try off-white instead of stark white.

Yellow

Red

Blue

Orange

Purple

Green

Illus. 20.

Illus. 21.

Illus. 22.

Oriental skin will blossom against poppy red. Use magenta and purple to soften sallow tones of the skin.

In general, brunette skin, eyes, and hair come alive when complemented by clear colors and strong contrasts. Large patterns, shiny or highly textured fabrics add to the drama of your look.

Color for Everyone

Complete your personal chart and isolate the color samples that represent your look: your best colors for clothing and accessory choices. Assemble these personal samples in three groups, just as you found them: hair, eye and skin colors. There are times when you might want to emphasize different features; separating the colors helps direct your decisions.

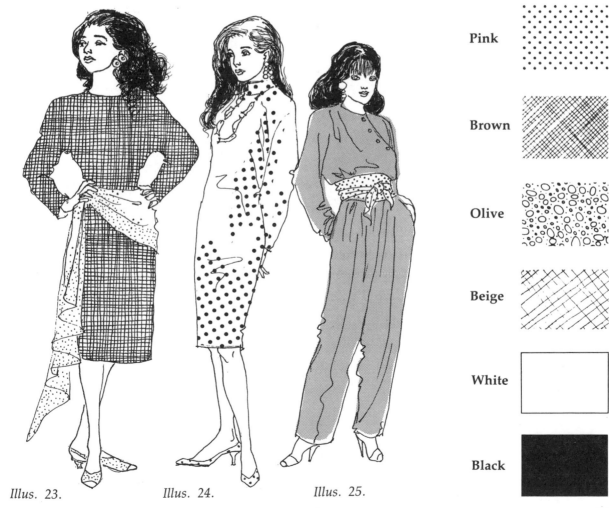

Illus. 23.   *Illus. 24.*   *Illus. 25.*

Pink

Brown

Olive

Beige

White

Black

Organize the color samples in an envelope or a small notebook for easy access and portability. Add some blank pages for memos: ideas for future sewing, shops where the people are most helpful, fabric more suited to other seasons, where to buy interesting and/or unusual patterns, and similar things.

Carry your color chart with you when you shop for fabric, make-up or ready-made clothing. It is an important visual aid for making the best choice before you make a purchase.

Study the color range of your current clothing and work out a sensible plan and time schedule for bringing the colors from your personal chart into the existing wardrobe. There is no need to toss everything from your closet that is outside your immediate color range. You don't have to start over with bare hangers. Incorporate your best colors into your existing wardrobe a little at a time while you slowly eliminate the items that seriously detract from your coloring and personality.

It's always exciting to make changes in your wardrobe but don't let the excitement carry you away. Complete your color analysis for sound, personal knowledge. Then, carefully reorganize your closet. Make plans, not impetuous purchases.

Suitable new colors can be introduced into your wardrobe without draining your pocketbook. Some very flattering colors might be collected from the midst of what is already hanging in your closet or tucked into a drawer. Additional colors can be introduced in easy-to-handle ways:

- Scarves, dickeys, collars and pieces of jewelry bring touches of complimentary colors near your face. Each will tone favorite garments of "iffy" colors turning them into more usable items.

- A silk scarf wrapped around the waistline of a dress or skirt that isn't the most flattering color can bring new life to that garment by toning it in your best direction.

- Add a transformation dickey in a workable color to tone down the conflict between non-workable skirts and blouses.

- A "good" colored blouse or sweater will allow a "bad" colored skirt to continue to give service in your wardrobe.

Visit your local fabric shop and try on an assortment of colors. Bring several bolts of fabric to a mirror and drape the yardage near your face. Try various tones or shades of the same color; look for texture changes, combine familiar colors with colors you've never tried before, and remember to return each bolt of fabric to its original home. That way you don't wear out your welcome.

There will be times when a color that is deemed a complete no-no works better than one that is supposed to be perfect for your complexion and general coloring. Temper all of the information you gather with your own good judgment. You know yourself and your likes, dislikes, and personality better than anyone. Have courage and faith in your personal perceptions—if you like it, wear it.

Jewelry has been mentioned several times as being an inexpensive way to introduce color into your wardrobe. We all have strands of beads, bracelets, etc., that we no longer wear. Paint pieces of costume jewelry with fingernail polish to achieve the new colors you're after. Nail polish is not only available in red, it comes in hundreds of shades of pink and brown as well as all the other colors of the rainbow—even black, white, navy blue, yellow and various shades of green. Try painting several strands of beads with nail polish of the prime colors from your chart. Twist the assortment of bead strings together for a low-cost start towards the new you.

Jewelry is also an important place to utilize the small scraps of fabric left over from sewing projects. "Quilted Jewelry" details some wonderful and inexpensive ways to experiment with color. Jewelry for neck, ears, and waist will add excitement to any wardrobe; you might even sew yourself a rainbow with assorted stripes of the colors listed in your chart.

Visit your local knitting shop and scan the shelves filled with hanks of yarn in beautiful colors and textures. Choose several skeins from the multitude and twist them into a collar or headband (Illus. 26). Braid several hanks of assorted yarns into a belt (Illus. 27). Pin the open ends together with a large brooch or tie on a decorative clasp or buckle. Close your yarn belt with a fabric flower. You'll enjoy this wonderful rainbow you've created in your personal colors.

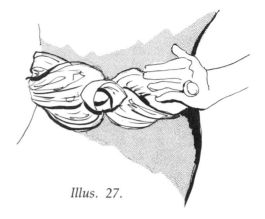

Illus. 27.

Illus. 26.

- Buy a pair of colored panty hose or tights to match a much-loved blouse or T-shirt. Can't find the right color? Dye your hose at home. Packets of nylon dye contain complete information for using the product.

- No shoes to wear with the new colored hose? A bottle of shoe paint can change an old pair of shoes from discards to wearable favorites in only a few minutes and the effect can be very striking. Your local department store or shoe repair shop can supply shoe paint in a huge variety of colors. The results are striking; a whole new outfit for a small investment.

- Wear a dickey under your suit jacket instead of a blouse. Choose several styles; make them up in assorted colors and fabrics; they work up faster than a complete blouse and are easier to pack or store.

- Drape a large scarf into a halter. It can add the touch of color you want and provide another change from the usual blouse. It also supplies a touch of glamour when the jacket comes off.

These are only a few ideas. You will probably come up with lots more (and better ones, too) if you give it some thought. Thumb through the pages of fashion magazines and look for the tricks they use to introduce color into their elegant photographs. Take note of the models with coloring similar to your own; check the colors and tones they're wearing in front of the camera. Notice what type of accessories they use to liven the whole look.

Wander into a local department store, find out which cosmetic companies are offering a make-up consultation and take advantage of their free promotion. This often includes a lot of good information on clothing color, as well. When all is said and done, make-up is still the icing on your personal cake. Much as this chapter generalizes on the use of color to include everyone, there is nothing like a hands-on, personal analysis from a working professional. With a wonderful world of color available for the asking, why not take advantage of it and put some sparkle into your life?

Always be willing to take a few color risks—your gain could be as much fun as "looking at the world through rose-colored glasses."

DICKEYS

You can wear your clothing as it comes off the sewing machine (which means that you must sew more garments than you can ever store) or you can make a selection of dickeys to change the appearance of your basics and extend the use of everything in your wardrobe (Illus. 28).

A dickey is a little bib or partial blouse that is worn under or over another garment. Sew them with a variety of necklines and you'll have a totally new view of your basic wardrobe; a whole new flavor to your dressing.

Once you wear dickeys you won't be able to get along without them. Slip a turtleneck dickey under a revealing V-neck sweater and it assumes a conservative neckline. A casual

Illus. 28.

T-shirt becomes suitable business wear when combined with a banded dickey. The same dickey can even fill in the deep neckline of a dinner dress making it acceptable daytime wear. Try a transformation dickey with a ruffled front over a very tailored dress and give it a soft, feminine look.

Finish a basic dickey with a banded neckline, turtleneck, cowl or conventional collar and you have an accessory that will put new excitement into too-familiar clothes. Dickeys relieve the boredom of clothing that you've over-worn, provide maximum clothing changes with minimum packing for business or pleasure trips, or just perk up the garments in your closet. Dressing is not dull when you include dickeys in your changing world.

The Basic Dickey Pattern

The overall measurements of both front and back of the basic dickey are 12 inches wide by 13 inches long. Sewn from knitted fabric that has built-in give, no alteration is necessary for the normal neckline opening to admit the head. Using woven fabric, a front or back opening is necessary to get the dickey on and off. The fabric you choose will determine the style and finish for each dickey.

Draft your basic dickey pattern with a one-piece front and back. No physical change is necessary to add an opening to the basic pattern, just fold the front or back segment along designated lines for cutting. A multitude of styles can be made up in any fabric with this pattern: cotton for a traditional look, silk or taffeta for a tailored but dressy look, or knits for anytime wear.

There are no mysterious formulae or complicated secrets to learn in order to create a dickey pattern: Just trace a few basic lines from a commercial shirt or tailored dress pattern and incorporate some personal measurements.

Separate the front, back, facings and collar segments from the pattern envelope, smooth them with a barely warm iron and lay these pattern pieces on your cutting board. Draw complete segments wherever possible, both right and left portions of the front and/or back. A complete pattern simplifies the cutting of special yardage where fabric designs or prints must be matched.

You'll need two sheets of pattern drafting cloth, tissue or nonwoven interfacing, each approximately 14 inches square, on which to draw the pattern for the basic dickey.

FRONT

1. Place tissue or pattern paper over the commercial pattern front. Draw a line for the center front down the middle of the pattern paper. Mark the top of the center line for the peak of the shoulders.

Measure down 13 inches along the center-front line and draw the line across the bottom edge for the hem (Illus. 29).

2. Measure and mark the width of the front segment, 12 inches evenly spaced across the center line.

3. Check the width and drop of the neck opening. It should measure approximately 5 inches wide with about a 3-inch drop. If the original neckline is suitable, trace it from the pattern; if not, adjust the opening to fit your measurements before you draw the lines on your pattern (Illus. 30).

4. Copy the shoulder line from the commercial pattern segment. Stay within your marked area: 6 inches from the center-front line, each side.

Connect the outside points of the shoulder with the hemline.

5. Trace the line of the overlap parallel to the center front. Note along this line: *Fold Line for Button Front, Cut Two.*

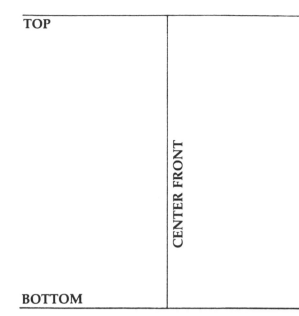

Illus. 29.

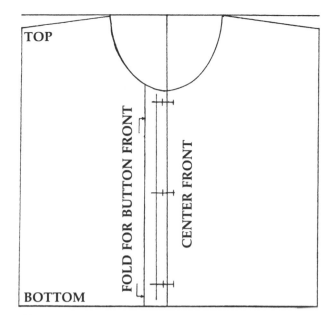

Illus. 31.

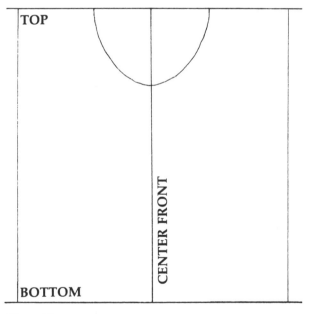

Illus. 30.

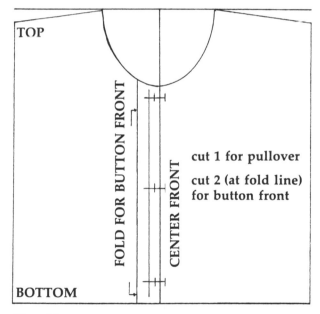

cut 1 for pullover

cut 2 (at fold line) for button front

Illus. 32.

Indicate the position of the buttons and buttonholes along the center-front line (Illus. 31). Space the buttons evenly, the top approximately ½ inch below the neckline, the lowest, 1 inch above the hem.

6. Complete the outline of the pattern front and label for identification: *Basic Dickey, Front. Cut One for Pullover, Cut on Fold Line for Two-Piece Front* (Illus. 32).

BACK

7.   Draw the center-back line down the middle of the pattern paper. Block in the overall dimensions of the back segment, using the length and total width measurements: 12 inches wide by 13 inches long. Indicate the measurements evenly across the center-back line (Illus. 33).

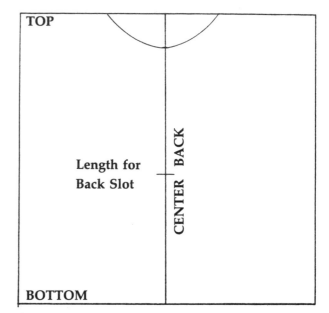

Illus. 34.

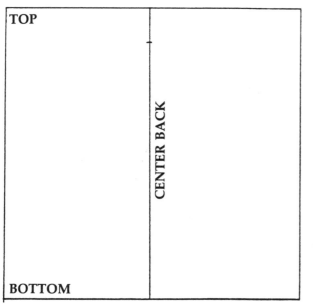

Illus. 33.

8.   Draw the back-neckline opening. It should be approximately 5 inches wide by 1½ inches deep (Illus. 34).

9.   Mark the shoulder lines and hem. Complete all pattern lines. Label the segment: *Basic Dickey, Back, Cut One* (Illus. 35).

COLLAR

If the original pattern has a curved collar, trace it and the facings onto another piece of the pattern paper. Mark the collar: *Cut Two, Interface.*

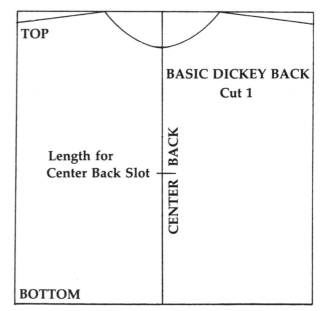

Illus. 35.

Collars don't always need patterns; some are cut as straight bands of fabric. This eliminates a separate pattern piece that can be mislaid. Just write the dimensions for your straight collar on the back pattern segment. Leave room on the pattern segment to note additional collar measurements. For example:

Straight Classic Collar: 16 inches by 6 inches.
Turtleneck: 16 inches by 6 inches
Banded neckline: 15 inches by 5 inches
Draped cowl: 21 to 23 inches by 12 to 20 inches in depth (The largest measurement for the cowl can become a hood.)

To use these neckline treatments, fold the pattern body slightly off-center (along the fold line) and cut a button-down style. The information for a conventional shirt collar is measured directly onto the fabric; no additional pattern pieces are necessary.

Use an envelope that is large enough to hold all the pieces of the pattern. If possible, match the size of other pattern envelopes in your file. Draw a picture of the basic dickey and alternate styles on the front of the envelope to identify the contents at a glance. Be sure each pattern segment is identified with its name: *Front, Back,* etc., and the date (to help keep your patterns current). Indicate that this pattern is suitable for any type of fabric, wovens or knits.

Basic Dickey Pattern from Measurements

The pattern for a basic dickey can be drafted from a few, simple measurements. Start with two sheets of pattern-drafting cloth or paper, approximately 14 inches square.

FRONT (see Illus. 29 through Illus. 32)

1.   Draw the center line for the front down the middle of the paper.

Mark the top for the peak of the shoulders. Indicate the 13-inch finished length of the dickey.

2.   At the top, space 12 inches evenly, across the center-front line for the width of the dickey base.

3.   Indicate the front neckline opening: 5 inches evenly spaced across the center line.

Measure the neckline drop for the front: 2½ to 3 inches below the top line of the pattern. Curve the line between the marked points, completing the neckline.

4.   Indicate a ¼-inch drop at the outside edge of the pattern for the slope of the shoulder line. Complete the shoulder line from the top of the neckline curve to the outside edge of the pattern.

5.   Connect the outer point of the shoulder line with the hem along the outside edge.

6.   Draw a second line, 1 inch to the left of the center line for the overlap of a two-piece front.

Space three marks evenly, along the center line to indicate the placement of buttons and buttonholes. Start ½ inch below the drop of the neckline for the top button. Mark for the lowest button 1 inch above the bottom hem edge. Label this line: *Cut Here for Two-Piece Front.*

7.   Mark the segment: *Front: Cut One for Pullover, Cut Two for Button Front.*

BACK (see Illus. 33 through Illus. 35)

8.   On the second piece of pattern paper, draw the center-back line down the middle of the page.

Mark the top and measure down 13 inches to the hem. Draw the line across the page.

Measure the 12-inch width across the center line and mark the outside edges.

9.   Draw the back neckline 1½ inches down from the top line, 4¾ to 5 inches across the center line. Draw the complete curve of the back neck opening.

10.   Indicate the shoulder drop ¼ inch down from the top, along the side-seam edge. Angle the shoulder lines from the edge of the neckline to the marked points at the side edges.

11.   Connect all unfinished lines for the pattern piece and identify the segment: *Basic Dickey Pattern, Back, Cut One*.

FACINGS AND COLLARS

A 2½-inch wide facing is adequate to support the buttons and buttonholes and keep the fronts of the dickey crisp. Trace the facings from the completed pattern.

FRONT FACING

1.   Fold the pattern front along the two-piece-front line.

2.   Trace across 2 to 3 inches of the hem edge, up the entire length of the center front and around the curve of the front neckline. Continue the line of the facing for 2½ inches of the shoulder line.

3.   Measure and mark the facing pattern for a consistent width. Complete all lines and label: *Front Facing, Cut Two*.

BACK FACING

4.   Trace the back-neckline curve and 2½ inches of the shoulder line, each side, for the back-neckline facing.

5.   Mark off several points, 2½ inches from the curve, and complete the outer line of the back facing. Label: *Back Facing, Cut One*.

Write the measurements for various collar styles on the back segment of the pattern where there are less lines and other information. Some dimensions have already been listed on this page. Copy the measurements you plan to use or write measurements for your own designs.

QUICK-SEW DETAILS

Dickeys sew up in no time. If you have a serger (overlock machine), use it for the entire dickey. With a conventional sewing machine only, use a serging stitch for the seams, a narrow zigzag stitch for the outside edges. You can also roll a narrow hem around the outside of the dickey or topstitch around the edges.

The following details are for a button-front dickey.

1.   Sew the shoulder seams, each side, with right sides together.

2.   Sew the *collar facing* to the neckline of the dickey base, right sides together.

3.   Sew the front and back neckline facings together at the shoulder seams.

4.   Attach the *top portion of the collar* to the neckline of the facing.

5.   Sew facings to dickey base, right sides together. Stitch completely around the outside edges of the collar, closing the seam.

6.   Overcast the entire outside of the dickey with the serger or roll a narrow hem all the way around and topstitch. Turn to right side.

7.   Complete buttonholes and sew on buttons.

Illus. 36.

Illus. 37.

Illus. 38.

Illus. 39.

Illus. 40.

Illus. 41.

Illus. 42.

Illus. 43.

The collar is the most important part of a dickey as it is the most visible. Vary the collar style or trim and you create an entirely new look for the basic pattern.

- Fringe around the outer edges (Illus. 36). A short fringe is tailored, a long fringe a little more ornamental. There are two basic approaches to fringing a collar:

- 1) Self-fringe: Sew a line of machine-stitching around the sew line of the collar, ¼ to ½ inch inside the raw edge. Draw threads from the fabric to the line of stitching to fringe, all the way around.

- 2) Add commercially-made fringe to the outside edge of the collar. Scw the woven edge between the collar top and facing.

- Add lace edging around the outside of any style collar (Illus. 37).

- Decorative edgings: There is a huge assortment of commercial edgings available in the notions department of your fabric shop. Embroidered ribbon, preruffled eyelet edging, rickrack, braids and laces of all varieties for you to try. If you don't find anything you like, make some edgings by machine-embroidering strips of fabric with your sewing machine cams (Illus. 38).

- Use a narrow strip of lace edging to finish the neckline; no collar (Illus. 39).

- Scallop the edges of the collars using a blind hemming stitch on your machine (Illus. 40). Run the straight stitch along the edge of the collar, the swing stitch just off the edge of the fabric. It will draw up soft fabric into a series of scallops.

- Make a 2-inch band for a mock-turtleneck look (Illus. 41). This is a nicely tailored finish. Back-slot opening, please, with woven fabrics. (Slash dickey back for 4 inches, from the neckline curve.)

35

• Sew a Peter Pan or Eton collar for the dickey base instead of a pointed collar (Illus. 42.).

Note: Make cuffs to match collars for a real change of pace (Illus. 43). They set a very different note for your outfit.

Cuffs

Measure the size of the opening at the bottom edge of the sleeve to determine the width of the cuff. Make the cuffs as deep as you wish, keeping them in the same general style as the collar (Illus. 43).

Illus. 44.

Tack the finished cuffs around the lower edge of each sleeve or use tiny safety pins to hold the cuffs in place temporarily. Insert one pin at the sleeve seam, one at the opposite side.

Even though sleeve openings are not always the same size, cuffs can be transferred to other garments. If they are too short to go completely around the new sleeve end and overlap, have the ends meet at the seam. Gather the sleeve along the hemline and use three small pins to hold the cuff in place: one for each end and the third pin to secure the cuff at the outside fold line. Overlap the ends of a cuff that is too long. Insert a small pin at the seam line (through all but the top layer of fabric) and one at the fold line of the sleeve to hold each cuff in place.

BRACELET CUFF

There is a non-traditional style of cuff that is fun to wear, consisting of a little ruff for the end of each sleeve (Illus. 44). It extends the fluffy look of a ruffled dickey and blends well with the more tailored ones. Make them from fabric to match a dickey, or try lace or tulle for self-contained units.

1. Cut two strips of fabric for each cuff, 4 inches wide by 12 inches long.

2. Finish the raw edges around each strip, if the fabric requires hemming.

3. Place the fabric together, wrong sides facing. Sew an elastic casing down the length of the fabric. Space two rows of stitching, approximately ¼ inch apart, or wide enough to admit a piece of elastic.

4. Thread 8 inches of ¼-inch elastic (or whatever it takes to wrap comfortably around the wrist without binding) through the casing and stitch the ends. The elastic will ruffle the fabric.

5. Sew the short ends of each strip together, forming two ruffled rings.

6. Complete the second cuff.
    Slip one ruffle over each wrist, just covering

the ends of a sweater or shirtsleeve. These cuffs are a very feminine transformation for simple garments.

Note: If you wear your hair long, try pulling it back into a pony tail or chignon. Wrap these elastic ruffles around your hair for a festive look.

Ruffled Dickey

Go feminine with ruffles. Tightly gathered and widely flounced, crisply pleated and rather tailored, with or without a collar, ruffles are an appealing finish for any style of dickey. A convertible neckline can be worn open, or you can close the neckline with thin ties or buttons (Illus. 45 and 46). Wear this dickey with a deep V-neck sweater or a casual jacket. The look is important—another strong statement.

Illus. 46.

Illus. 45.

WITH A COLLAR

1. Use the Basic Dickey Pattern to cut the body of the dickey. Fold the front segment of the pattern along the appropriate line and cut two. The back is cut in one piece. You will also need facings for the front and the back neckline.

2. Cut a two-piece collar, straight or shaped. The ruffle is inserted between the segments: outer portion and facing.
    A straight collar is approximately 2 inches wide, 16 inches long. This size is just right to wear standing up or folded flat around the shoulders.
    Don't forget the seam allowance.

3. Hem and gather enough 1-inch ruffling to go completely around the collar and down the front opening. If the fronts overlap (button front), don't ruffle the under-portion as it is too bulky. If the fronts meet and tie, ruffle all the way around the opening.

4. Sew the shoulder seams between the front and back. Attach the collar facing around the neckline.
    Turn a narrow hem around the outside edges of the dickey and topstitch or sew on the serger.

5. Complete the shoulder seams of the facings.
    Stitch the top portion of the collar to the facings, at the neckline.

6. Place the facing over the outer portion of the dickey, right sides together. Pin the ruffle around the collar and down the front of the opening, between the body of the dickey and the facing. Stitch around the edge, securing all three layers. Turn right side out.

7. Add buttons and complete the buttonholes.

WITHOUT A COLLAR

1. Cut the body and facings for the dickey with a front-slot opening, using the Basic Dickey Pattern.

2. Hem and gather enough 2-to-3-inch wide ruffling to go completely around the neckline and opening at the front (approximately one and one-half to twice the measurement of the length to be covered).

3. Complete the outside hem around the dickey.

4. Pin the gathered edge of the ruffling between the body of the dickey and the facing, around the neckline and down the front. Sew.

5. Make two string ties approximately 12 inches long. Fold one end of each tie and tack securely to the inside point of the neckline, each side (Illus. 46). Knot the bottom end. Tie in a bow to close the neckline of the dickey.

Dickey with Pleated Neckband

Make a dickey with a pleated, stand-up collar (Illus. 47). Horizontal tucks add texture around the neckline, a slot opening at the back makes for easy access.

The pleated neckband dickey style is adaptable to an assortment of fabrics: voile, men's shirting, broadcloth, brocade, faille, satin, solid color, stripe or print. It can be made from as little as a quarter of a yard of fabric. Hooks and eyes, snaps or buttons close the back neckline.

DIRECTIONS

1. Use the Basic Dickey Pattern for this design. Cut the front in one piece, the back with a 4-inch slit for the neckline extension.

Illus. 47.

2. Assemble the body of the dickey, hem the outside edges and serge the slot opening.

COLLAR

3. Cut the collar band approximately 7 inches wide by 16½ inches long. (The band should be long enough to go completely around your neck, include a seam allowance at each end, and not bind when closed at the back.)

4. Fold down four ¼-inch pleats along the length of the fabric, starting approximately ½ inch from one long side. Topstitch each pleat to hold it in place.

5. Fold the pleated neckband in half, parallel to the pleats and pin in a ¼-inch seam allowance at each end. Stitch ends on a conventional machine or blindstitch by hand.

6. Fold back a narrow facing along the back-slot opening. Sew the band around the neckline of dickey base using an overlock machine. Tie off the ends of the thread.

7. Hand- or machine-stitch two hooks and eyes or snaps to the neckband: one set to the top of the collar below the top pleat, the second set at the seam of the collar and body.

Note: When using striped or patterned material, be sure to plan the dickey in keeping with the pattern of the fabric. All pleats should be evenly spaced parallel to the stripes of the fabric, all stripes equal on each pleat.

Variation: Arrange the dickey base with vertical stripes, neckband horizontal.

Pleated Dickey

The pleated-front dickey is another highly wearable insert that goes well with almost any garment (Illus. 48). Either draw a new pattern front to enlarge the Basic Dickey Pattern (to include the pleats) or create the pleats on an uncut piece of fabric and cut the neckline opening later. The following directions tell you how to plan enough fabric for the front pleats. There are no changes to the back portion of the pattern.

The pattern front includes seven pleats: five within the neckline curve (a box pleat at the center with two knife pleats, each side), plus one knife pleat either side of the center-front pleating. The measurements of the pleats are added to the width of the Basic Dickey Pattern.

The easiest way to handle multiple pleating is to pre-pleat the fabric and then cut the neckline evenly across the center front (Illus. 49).

Illus. 48.

Carefully mark the fabric and sew all pleats even and parallel. Each pleat is stitched down over the fold for the reverse.

1. Cut a rectangular piece of fabric 17 inches wide by 13 inches long.

2. At the center of the 17-inch side mark a 1-inch space for the top of the box pleat. Indicate a ½-inch return on each side. Work in one direction at a time to keep the continuity of the pleating.

3. Leave a 1-inch space for the next pleat and mark the ½-inch return. Repeat twice more for a total of three knife pleats beside the center box pleat.

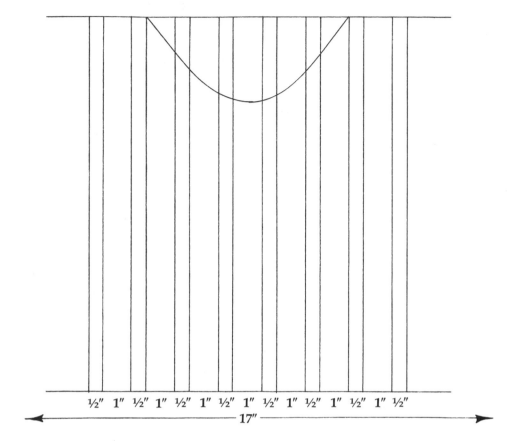

½" 1" ½" 1" ½" 1" ½" 1" ½" 1" ½" 1" ½" 1" ½"

← —————————————— 17" —————————————— →

Illus. 49.

4. Measure three knife pleats (surface and return) for the other half of the front, next to the center box pleat.

5. Fold and topstitch each pleat over the reverse.

6. When all pleats are stitched, mark the 5-inch wide by 3-inch-deep neckline opening across the front, centering the neckline drop over the middle box-pleat. Cut along the marked line.

7. Use either a plain neckband or a pleated one (see "Dickey With Pleated Neckband") and complete the dickey with a back-slot opening.

Sew snaps or hooks and eyes to the edges of the band: one set at the top, one set at the seam line of the dickey base and the collar.

Dickeys from Knitted Fabric

Make turtleneck dickeys from knit fabrics in about fifteen minutes (Illus. 50). Three little pieces; three short seams to sew. They're wonderful under sweaters, sweatshirts and T-tops as they blend well with other knit fabrics.

This style is also cut from the Basic Dickey Pattern. Front and back are one-piece segments. No additional openings or extensions of the neckline are necessary as knitted fabric has built-in stretch and these turtlenecks can be pulled over the head.

1. Place your Basic Dickey Pattern on the fabric and cut one back, one front.

Illus. 50.

Transformation Dickey

A transformation dickey is one that is worn over the top of another garment, much like a tabard or vest without sides. It is held to the belt with fabric loops that are sewn into the hem edge, both front and back (Illus. 51). Make a Transformation Dickey from a single piece of face fabric (with a lining) or sew double, from contrasting fabric, for a reversible dickey that gives twice the service.

Draft a separate pattern for this dickey as the dimensions are totally different from anything you've already made.

Illus. 51.

2. Measure and cut a straight turtleneck collar 16 inches by 10 inches. The collar can be cut horizontally, vertically or on the bias.

3. Sew the shoulder seams of the base on the serger.

4. Match the short ends of the collar, right sides together, and sew into a ring. Fold the ring down, right side out, and pin the doubled fabric to the base, evenly spaced around the neckline opening. Sew in place on your overlock machine.

5. Serge completely around the outside of the dickey. Slip the finished dickey over your head and fold the collar down to a comfortable level.

FRONT (Illus. 52)

1. Draw the center-front line down the middle of the pattern paper.

Mark the top for the peak of the shoulder-line.

2. Trace the *shoulder* and *necklines* from the Basic Dickey Pattern, evenly spaced across the center line.

3. Along the center line, sketch a mark 4 inches below the bottom edge of the neckline: the depth for a front-slot opening. (This dickey can open front or back so both segments will be marked.) Label the line: *"Front Neckline Opening."*

4. Measure your length from shoulder to waistline at the front (approximately 18 to 19 inches). Extend a measuring tape to this length for the front pattern segment and draw the hemline across the pattern.

5. Evenly space an 8-inch measurement across the center line at the hem. This is the front width at the hemline and should be varied to suit your personal measurements.

Angle a line from the outer point of the shoulder to meet the marked width for the hem, each side.

Label the segment: *Transformation Dickey, Front, Cut One.*

BACK (Illus. 53)

6. Draw the center line down the middle of the paper and mark for the top of the pattern back.

7. Trace the back neckline and shoulders from the Basic Dickey across the top of the pattern.

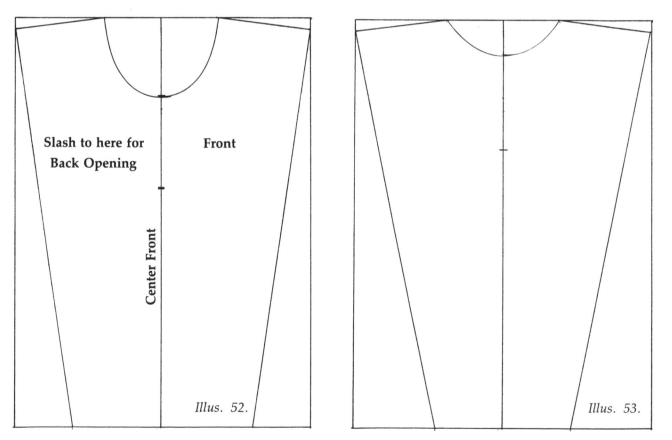

Slash to here for Back Opening

Front

Center Front

Illus. 52.

Illus. 53.

8. Measure and mark a point 4 inches below the center of the back neckline for a back-slot opening. (A front or back opening is optional; both should be marked.) Identify the line to prevent future errors: *Back Neckline Opening.*

9. Extend the back segment of the pattern to approximately the same length as the front (18 to 19 inches) and mark for the hem.

10. The width at the hem edge of the back segment is 6 inches, evenly spaced across the center line . (Adjust this measurement to suit.) Connect the outer points of the shoulders with the hemline.

11. You need six loops to hold the dickey to your belt but you don't need an additional pattern piece for them. Note on one pattern segment: *Cut Strip from Selvage for Six Loops:* 1½ inches wide by 24 inches long.

COLLAR

The Transformation Dickey will adapt to any number of different collar styles. List the measurements for all straight-cut collars directly on one segment of the pattern; draw separate pattern pieces for shaped collars.

Detail whether the straight collars, ties and scarves are for front or back opening neckline treatments. Several collar styles are listed in the section on the Basic Dickey. Write the information for each style on your Transformation Dickey Pattern along with a few more:

Straight Collar: 16 inches long by 5 to 7 inches wide.
Narrow Tie: 28 inches long by 4 inches wide.
String Ties for Front Closure: 12 inches for each bow, not more than 1¾ inches wide.

Turtlenecks, mock turtles and banded styles can take a back zipper or slot opening. Include the measurements for an optional placket to complete the slot opening at the front of the dickey.

SEWING INFORMATION

There are several ways to sew the Transformation Dickey to produce either a reversible or lined accessory. However you get there, the entire piece, shell and backing, is completely enclosed around all outside edges.

Six fabric loops are necessary to the finished dickey, so sew them first. Stitch the 1½-by-24-inch strip of fabric into a long tube with a ¼-inch seam. Turn to the right side. Cut the strip into six equal lengths. When attached to the dickey, these fabric loops are big enough to slide over a belt and hold the overgarment in place.

Cut the 4-inch slot opening down the center of the dickey front.

METHOD #1

1. Sew the shoulder seams of the outer shell.

2. Sew the shoulder seams of the facing.

3. Pin the shell and lining with right sides together. Machine-stitch just the slot opening at the neckline. Reinforce the lowest point. Do not stitch around the entire neckline as the garment will be turned to the right side through this opening.

4. Pin the six loops along the short hemlines, evenly spaced: three at the front and the remaining three at the back. The raw ends of each loop are facing out, the rounded portion is laid over the fabric between the outer shell and lining.

5. Sew completely around the outside of the dickey, turning the fabric carefully when you come to the corners, keeping each one square. Backtack over each loop to reinforce the stitching. Snip away the excess fabric at each corner.

6. Turn to the right side through the neckline opening.

7. Fold in a narrow seam allowance around the neckline. Pin the finished collar between the shell and the lining and topstitch.

METHOD #2

A collar or band around the neckline can be attached during the construction of the dickey, rather than as a separate unit.

1. Sew the shoulder seams of both shell and lining.

2. Pin and sew the collar *facing* to the neckline of the outer shell, right sides together.

3. Pin the collar *top* to the neckline of the lining, right sides together, and sew.

4. If you are finishing your dickey with a ruffle, hem the fabric along one side. On the opposite long side, run the gathering thread.
   Pin the ruffle between the collar and facing.
   Sew completely around the outside edges of the collar and around the slot opening, joining the outer shell and the lining (or inner shell), around the neckline.

5. Pin three folded loops, evenly spaced, along the front hem, three at the back. The loops are sandwiched between the two layers of fabric, folded end in, raw ends pointing out. Make sure you've left enough length on the loops for them to slip over your belts.

6. Sew around the outside edge of the dickey leaving a small opening along one side to turn the fabric.
   Turn the dickey to the right side.

7. Close the turning slot.
   Complete the buttonholes and buttons or other closure.

ASCOT NECKBAND

Finish the Transformation Dickey with an ascot instead of a conventional collar at the neck (Illus. 54). It can be sewn as a separate scarf, tacked to the neckline at the center back or sewn into the neckline during construction.

Illus. 54.

• The Ascot Tie for a *non-reversible* dickey is made from a single strip of fabric 10 to 12 inches wide by approximately 30 inches long. It is tacked to the finished neckline of the dickey.
   Sew the fabric into a tube with right sides together. Stitch across the ends and up the long side, leaving an opening at the center of the long seam through which to turn the fabric. Turn, press and tack the center of the seamed edge of the scarf to the neckline, at the center back.

• The ascot for a *reversible* dickey should also be reversible for consistency of the accessory.
   Cut a strip 5 to 7 inches wide by 30 inches long from each of the two fabrics used for the body of the dickey.
   Sew around the four sides of the scarf, leaving a small opening to turn the fabric. Tack the center of one long side to the center back of the dickey. Wrap from the back, looping the ends at the front.

MORE VARIATIONS

- A *Banded Neckline* is another finish for the transformation dickey. A 16-inch strip of fabric will fit comfortably around the neck. But you can vary the style by cutting a 22-inch-wide strip, 18 to 20 inches high, creating a draped cowl. This is wide enough to pull over the head with no additional opening at the neckline. Cut 1 to 2 inches deeper all around the neckline of the base to fit the collar to the dickey.

- Buttonholes aren't the only way to close a neckline: try loops of elastic, a very satisfactory substitute.

- Make your transformation dickey from a single piece of firm fabric such as duck, twill or ticking. Use corduroy or wool to match a skirt for another look. Firm fabrics need very little support but for a more professional look to the inside of your garments, a light lining or backing is essential.

Scarves

Scarves have been in fashion since the beginning of time. Simple squares and rectangles were the basis of the clothing of all early civilizations. In ancient Egypt, Greece, and Rome they were the robes of Nefertiti, the togas of the Caesars and the veils of Salome. In China and Japan, the kimono (both short and long), the obi, and all undergarments were styled from the same simple squares and rectangles (Illus. 55).

Illus. 55.

The apron also evolved from the scarf or square. It was a piece of cloth that was wrapped around the body and tied in place with a cord. Later, the apron came to signify the occupation of an individual, and the quality of the fabric used designated one's station in life.

At the same time, the double-wrapped stock was a popular item of neckwear for the well-dressed male. The stock, a long scarf or oversized ascot, was the forerunner of the man's tie we know today. Scarves are valued as much for their service as they are for fashion.

Scarves not only extend a wardrobe by accessorizing the basics, they can actually substitute for major items of clothing. Use a scarf to fill a neckline, add color and dash to a costume, or keep your shoulders warm (Illus. 56). Turn a large scarf into a halter, a dress, or a skirt. Use it to cover a bathing suit or define a waistline. Scarves can do wonderful things for your wardrobe while taking very little storage space.

There are no rules governing the size or shape of a scarf. A scarf is square, round, rectangular, triangular or free form. It drapes, gathers or folds over any part of your body. Tie a scarf in a knot or bow, clip or pin the ends with a brooch, or secure it by pulling the ends through a ring.

A well-chosen scarf can set the tone of your entire personal statement. A scarf is as small as 20-inches square (barely tying around the neck), as generous as 60-to-75 inches to cover the entire body—or anything in between. There are any number of varieties to spice up your accessory wardrobe; you might even create some styles of your own.

Scarves work up fast, and can be worn immediately. Here is some general information on sizes and shapes to inspire your scarf collection.

Illus. 56.

47

SQUARE

- A 24-to-26 inch square is a comfortable size for a neck kerchief. Tie it under a collar or drape it loosely over the neckline of a collarless bodice for a splash of color (Illus. 57). For a change of pace, overlap the ends and secure with a decorative pin or brooch.

Illus. 57.

Illus. 58.

- Use a 26-to-28-inch square for a head kerchief. It is large enough to comfortably cover the head and tie in a variety of ways; small enough to wear without it getting in your way (Illus. 58).

- A 36-inch square is perfect for a small shoulder cover. It can also be draped around your waist like a cummerbund or worn around the neckline of your bodice (Illus. 59).

- Opt for a 42-to-60-inch square (or more) and you have a scarf that is large enough to wear as a major item of clothing such as a dress or skirt (Illus. 60).

Illus. 59.

50

Illus. 60.

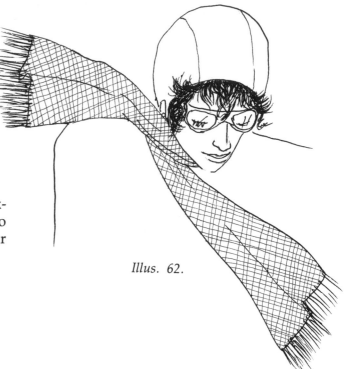

Illus. 62.

RECTANGULAR

• A rectangle 4-to-12 inches wide by approximately 36 inches long makes a nice ascot to loop around your neck inside your collar (Illus. 61).

• A rectangle 12 inches by 60 inches with fringed ends is called an aviator's scarf. World War I flying aces adopted this symbol of elan, wrapped around the neck and streaming behind them in the wind (Illus. 62).

Illus. 61.

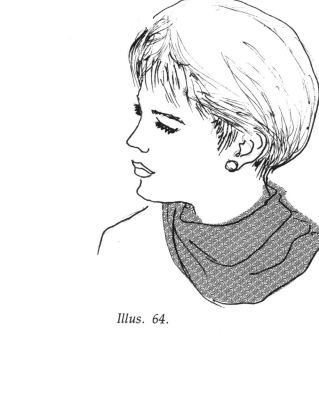

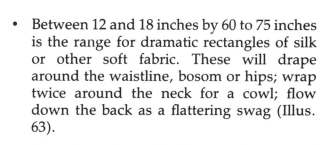

Illus. 64.

Illus. 63.

- Between 12 and 18 inches by 60 to 75 inches is the range for dramatic rectangles of silk or other soft fabric. These will drape around the waistline, bosom or hips; wrap twice around the neck for a cowl; flow down the back as a flattering swag (Illus. 63).

- A small scarf can also be sewn into a cowl shape (Illus. 64). It can match your bodice or contrast with it. A rectangle 20 by 24 inches is stitched into a ring, matching the 20-inch ends. Hem the circle, slip it over your head, and drape the fabric into attractive folds.

ROUND

- Make a small round, an 8-to-10-inch circle of silk, nylon or rayon to drape gracefully from the pocket of a jacket, blouse or skirt instead of the traditional square handkerchief. Hem the circle on the serger, by hand, or appliqué lace around the outside edge.

- Round scarves can be used as jabots (Illus. 65). They are elegant when worn at the neck of a tailored shirt. Pin at the collar band with a fancy brooch or pin, just covering the top button. Very attractive finish for the neckline.

Illus. 66.

Illus. 65.

- Place a small, lace-trimmed round (approximately 6 inches in diameter) on your head for those moments when some sort of covering is essential (Illus. 66).

- Cut a full circle, the width of a drapable piece of fabric, and the result is a beautiful cape-like shawl to wear over anything (Illus. 67). For sheers, the trim should be lightly scaled: plain or metallic lace edging, matching or contrasting eyelet edging, silk fringe or simply a rolled hem. Heavier yardage such as wool or cotton challis, fine knits, jerseys or handwovens can be finished with yarn fringe, embroidered ribbon or bias binding of cotton, lace or leather.

TRIANGLES

- A triangular scarf serves much the same purpose as a square. Cut a square in half, on the bias, any time you want to eliminate some of the bulk from a scarf. When you want a head scarf that hugs the skull, a hip wrap that stays close to the body, or where you always fold a scarf into a triangle and would just as soon share half the fabric with someone else, cut the fabric in half and make two scarves. The long side of the triangle should be at least 24 inches to tie.

ASSORTED HEMS AND FINISHES

There are many attractive ways to finish a scarf. Some are very fast and easy; others take a little time and patience, each becomes a distinctive look.

1. *Square, rectangular, triangular or round:* Roll a narrow hem (⅛ inch) all the way around and sew with concealed hand-stitching. Picking a hem takes time, but when working with lovely fabric, such as silk or sheer wool, it's always worth the extra effort.

2. *Square:* Take a ½-to 1½-inch hem on all four sides and mitre the corners. Hand- or machine-sew. Double-wide hems look particularly handsome on sheer fabrics.

3. *Square or rectangular:* Turn the hem up, over the face of the fabric. Hand- or machine-stitch decorative braid or fancy ribbon over the raw edges.

4. *Rectangular:* Roll hems and hand stitch the long sides. Self-fringe the short sides by pulling threads across the grain.

5. *Rectangular:* Take a narrow hem (approximately ⅛ inch) on the long sides, 1 inch or more along the short ends.

6. *All styles:* Use a serger (overlock machine) to finish the edges on all four sides. This is a neat, simple and fast finish for "less important" fabrics.

7. *All styles:* Stitch a narrow rolled hem all the way around with a conventional sewing machine.

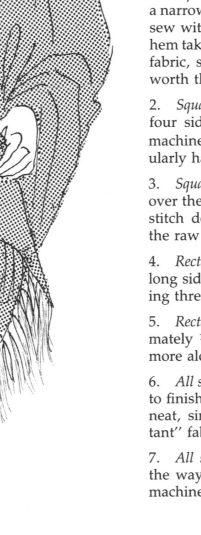

Illus. 67.

8.   *All styles:* Appliqué lace around the entire scarf. Sew the lace edging to the fabric with a narrow zigzag stitch. Go around all four sides. Trim the excess fabric to the line of stitching without cutting the threads.

9.   *All styles:* Look for interesting allover prints. Use the serger to roll a narrow hem around the fabric, following the lines of the printed pattern. This method can result in some interesting, free-form shapes.

NOTES ON WEARING A SQUARE

• Fold a 24-to-36-inch scarf on the bias (Illus. 68), bring the two corners around the back of your neck, and tie in a small knot at the nape (Illus. 69). Allow the center points to hang over the front of the bodice, adding a splash of color to your costume, providing a soft cowl effect.

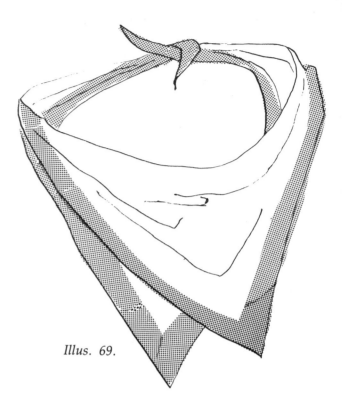

Illus. 69.

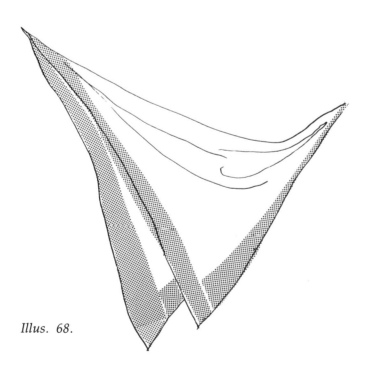

Illus. 68.

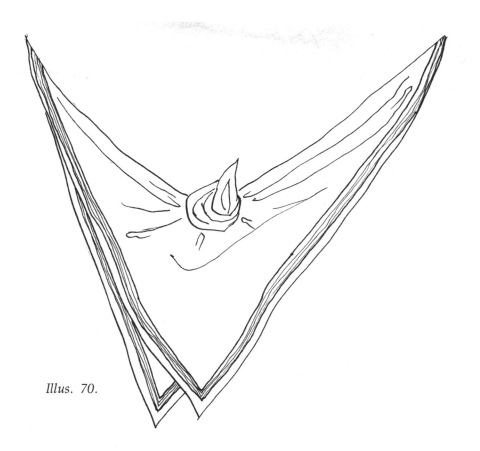

Illus. 70.

- There are other ways to tie a scarf into the soft drape of a cowl. Fold the square into a triangle and tie a knot at the center to weight it (Illus. 70). Drop the knot inside the neckline of your bodice. Take two opposing corners, bring them around to the back, and tie at the nape of the neck. The back knot can rest outside the neckline or be tucked into the neckband.

- Fold a 24-to-36-inch square on the bias, hang the points at the front, and drape the bias ends around the neck, crossing them at the back. Double-wrap, returning the ends to the front where they are tied into a knot (Illus. 71). Turn the folded edge over to conceal the knot: the look of a turtleneck shirt under a jacket or sweater.

- For an attractive shawl, fold a 36-inch square (or larger) on the bias and knot the ends over one shoulder. Allow the point to drape over the opposite shoulder.

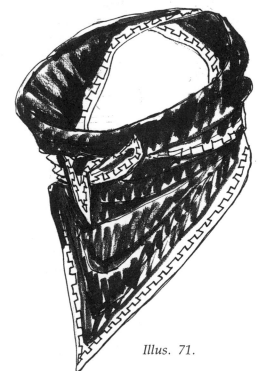

Illus. 71.

57

- Wear a medium-size square as a sash. Fold the opposite ends over the center, fold a second time narrowing the width to a workable size and padding the center so it will stay in place without crushing (Illus. 72). Tie from front to back, tuck the ends under.

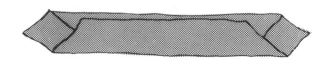

Illus. 72.

- Fold an extra-large square as explained. Wrap to the back, then bring the ends around to the front. Twist the points together in front and tuck the ends into the twist for another obi-look (Illus. 73).

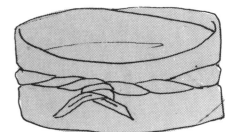

Illus. 73.

- For the most wonderful, wearable halter: Fold a 36-inch scarf on the bias. Take one center point in each hand and knot behind your neck (Illus. 74). Wrap the bias ends to the back and tie near the waistline (Illus. 75). If the ends are long enough, return them to the front and tie. Adjust all knots for your comfort.

  The neckline can be worn modestly high or low and daring. The style works with large or small scarves, looks good under a jacket or on its own. In summer: wear pretty cotton squares with matching skirts; in winter: lightweight wool challis, brocades, jacquards, any fabric suitable to the occasion for which you're dressing.

Illus. 74.

Illus. 75.

ADDITIONAL USES FOR LARGE SQUARES

- In warm weather a large scarf can be worn as a tropical style sarong. Wrap a large square from back to front, high under the arms. Take the two ends and twist two or three times. Separate the ends and either tie around the back of the neck or tuck the ends into the top of the bodice.

  Another way to tie a wrapped dress is: Twist the ends two or three times and wrap them around the knot, forming a rose. Pull the last of the end through the center of the twist and open like a leaf (Illus. 76). This is an elegant tie for any scarf.

  For a more covered look: Hold the scarf square. Place the center of one edge under your arm. Take the ends across your body to the opposite shoulder, twisting each end in once or twice, towards your arm. Tie over the shoulder (Illus. 77).

Illus. 77.

Illus. 76.

- In colder weather you can drape a large-size challis scarf over a body stocking (or leotard and tights) as a skirt. Place the center of one side of the square at your waistline, just over one hip. Pull the ends towards the opposite hip, twisting once to drape the fabric. Tie in a knot or single bow.

- Crush a large scarf and wrap it around the waist leaving one end to hang as long as possible. Tie a knot with the short end and open the swag for a lovely drape that will cascade down your side (Illus. 78).

- Secure the scarf at the shoulder with a large pin or brooch (Illus. 79). The loose ends can be pulled to the opposite side and tied, or just left hanging, as you please.

  Drape a large square over one shoulder, but put a small safety pin through the scarf, under a fold of the fabric, to keep it in place. Use your brooch to secure the ends at the waist or hip.

  Slide a scarf through the epaulet of a shirt or jacket and tie the ends near the waist at the opposite side (Illus. 80). You can do the same thing without the epaulets; just use a little pin.

  Another choice: With epaulets, slip a scarf through the opening and allow it to hang down, front and back (Illus. 81). Nice way to perk-up a garment.

All of the above scarf styles are for multiple use; the following designs will limit the use of your scarf to a single purpose, but each is a style well worth sewing.

Illus. 78.

Illus. 79.

Illus. 80.

Illus. 81.

Padded Head Scarf

Finish the hem of a 24-to-28-inch scarf from a fabric of your choice: cotton, rayon, polyester or silk; prints, stripes or solid colors. You might even want to try a pre-printed fabric square. They come in a variety of attractive patterns: scenic, geometric, floral or animal prints. Most come with printed borders; some can be cut along an assortment of lines to alter the size of the finished scarf.

In addition to the fabric, you need a strip of polyfoam approximately 3 by 5 inches. Don't use anything too thick or it won't shape to your head—about ⅛ inch thick will do it—along with matching or contrasting thread.

Fold the finished scarf on the bias, forming a triangle. Place the piece of polyfoam between the layers of the folded scarf and stitch two lines parallel to the fold line to keep the foam pad in place.

Wear the scarf with the folded edge draped over the head, the ends tied into a knot at the nape of the neck (Illus. 82). This scarf will stay right where you put it.

Illus. 82.

Turban

There are times when any woman feels she must hide her hair from public view. Wear this helmet-like turban, made from a 26-to-28-inch square. It will solve the problem.

1. Fold the finished scarf into a triangle.

2. Place the folded edge across your forehead and bring the ends to the back, over the points of the scarf (Illus. 83).

3. Cross the ends at the back of your head and bring them towards the front (Illus. 84).

4. Tie a knot over one ear with the short length; twist the long length into a rope (Illus. 85). Wrap the long, twisted end around the knot, forming a flower. Tuck the end under and through the center of the twist.

Wrap the back points around the twisted band at the back.

Illus. 83.

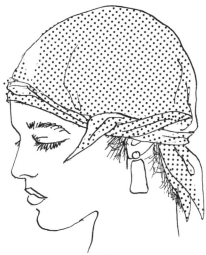

Illus. 84.

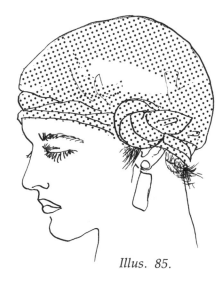

Illus. 85.

- Try a flower-twist to secure a small square at the neck of your shirt, or at the waistline with a long rectangle. This little trick can be used with any size of scarf. It can be tied at any point around your head—a lovely way to secure a pretty scarf. A second scarf can be twisted into a rope and wrapped around the turban for an additional touch of color. Tie the ends near the knot of the first square and double the flower-power.

Fishnet Triangle

Cut a triangle from coarse fishnet and trim with strips of leather, Ultrasuede or fabric.

1. Bias-fold 30 to 36 inches of fishnet (heavy cotton or synthetic yarn mesh). Cut the triangle along the fold of the fabric. It will not be an equilateral triangle as fishnet is approximately 54 inches wide. The beauty of these scarves is in the trim.

Leather: Use leather or suede (synthetic or natural) to complete the borders and a center design.

Cut irregular rectangles to border the edges of the scarf. This will enhance the uneven shape of the fishnet. A decorative motif is topstitched at the center of the scarf (Illus. 86). Hems or edge-finishes are not necessary for leather.

Cut the border in small segments if you are short of leather scraps. Piece to fit around the edges of the triangle.

Fabric: Use woven or knitted fabric for the finishing details. Unlike leather, woven and knitted fabrics must be edge-finished. Turn under all raw edges as you topstitch fabric to the mesh or use a satin stitch to prevent raveling.

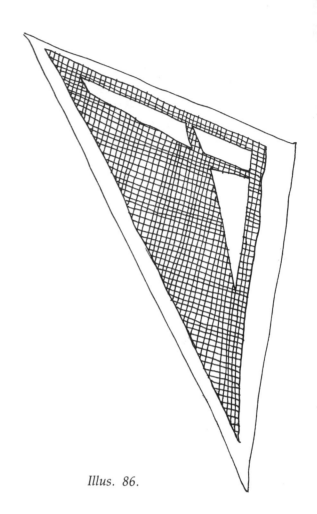

Illus. 86.

2. *Finishing details:* Fold a narrow hem around the triangle, over the face of the mesh. Place the leather, suede or fabric on top of the folded edge and topstitch the trim in place to hide the raw edges of the fishnet.

Cut a design of rectangles or free-form shapes for the center of the scarf and topstitch in place.

Make several of these fishnet scarves. Trim the collection to match pants, skirts or jackets. They can pull odd separates together and round out your wardrobe. Drape one or more around your neck and either tie the ends in a knot or use a fancy pin or clip to secure.

Lettuce Edge Ruffled Jabot

Although this ruffled tie isn't a true triangle, it's close enough to be included with triangular scarves. The finished look of a leaf-edged jabot will accent neckline, hipline or hemline, or add a soft note to your most tailored blouses or shirts (Illus. 87).

Use this method of lettuce-leaf hemming to top off anything from yards of ruffled edging for the bottom of a skirt to little detailing for accessory pieces. You will find it an elegant finish for lingerie, nightwear, blouses, dresses and/or evening apparel. But do practice the technique involved in ruffling fabric edges before you try it on an almost-finished garment; it's a little tricky the first time out.

Illus. 87.

JABOT

There are two basic ways of cutting the fabric for the jabot:

(a) Three bias strips of matching length: 4 inches wide by 14 inches long, or

(b) Three bias strips of varied lengths: 12 inches, 15 inches, 19 inches, each 4 inches wide.

1. Cut the fabric for the jabot in the manner of your choosing.

2. Overcast the edges on a serger or with a zigzag stitch of a conventional sewing machine. Stretch the fabric edge as you sew keeping enough tension along the edge to ripple the line of stitching. The result is the lettuce-leaf effect that is so flouncy.

3. Sew all strips to points at each end.
    Allow the fabric to drape and/or twist, just as it comes off the machine (Illus. 88).

4. Whipstitch the center of all three ties to a small safety pin. The puffiness of the fabric will hide the pin.

The ruffles will cascade down the front of your shirt or blouse or hang nicely at your hipline.

Rectangular Scarves

The size of a scarf is a matter of personal preference, whatever the shape. The size of a rectangular is judged by whether there is enough length to drape around the neck, waist or hips, loop in front and have enough fabric left at the ends to keep it from untying. The width should be enough to suit you.

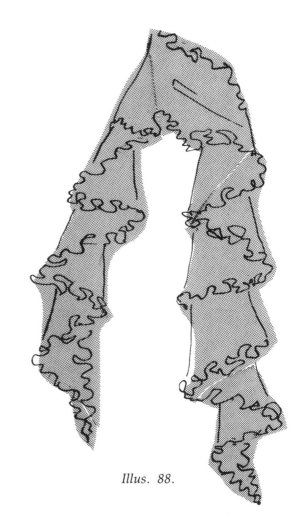

Illus. 88.

In the smaller rectangular scarf category there is the ascot. It is a very traditional sort of scarf that has been popular for centuries.

66

Ascot

An ascot is a scarf that is approximately 30 to 36 inches long and as wide as 10 to 12 inches at each end. A tuck across the center controls the width, allowing the ascot to seat comfortably at the nape of the neck (Illus. 89).

Any soft fabric suitable for ties or scarves can be made into an ascot. Knitted or woven fabric in solid colors or white, stripes of any description, or small prints adapt well to this style. This little scarf can be made from approximately ¼ yard of fabric or less. You'll also need a spool of matching thread.

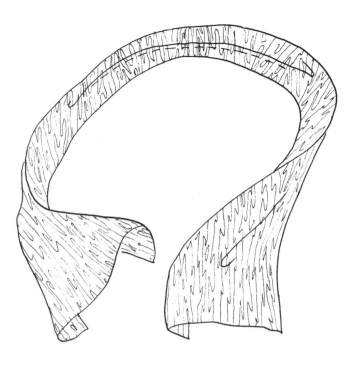

Illus. 89.

DIRECTIONS

An ascot can be cut with the grain of the fabric running in any direction; the choice is yours. This can be important if you are looking at "pricey" fabric. You can save material by cutting across the grain. Use as little as 6 inches of actual yardage length by 36 inches or the total width of the fabric.

If you are cutting a garment from a large piece of fabric, cut the ascot anywhere it fits into the layout of the pattern: cross-grain, with the grain, or even on the true bias, all ways work.

METHOD #1

1. Cut a 10-to-18-inch strip of fabric across the grain, the width of the material (at least 36 inches). This is a luxuriously full ascot (or stock) that can be double-wrapped for a different look.

2. Fold the strip lengthwise, right sides together, and sew into a long tube.

3. Turn the scarf to the right side, centering the seam down the middle of the tube and press.

4. Fold in a ¼-inch hem allowance at either end and catch-stitch the ends in place. (The hems may also be finished by any of the methods mentioned earlier in this segment.)

5. Take a 1-to-2-inch tuck, down the length, across the center of the completed tie to shape the neckband. The actual depth of the tuck will be determined by the finished width of the ascot.

Machine-stitch the pleat for approximately 8 to 10 inches.

There is another method for making an ascot that is quite effective. When worn, this second style of ascot has a more luxurious appearance because of the extra fullness at the overlapped ends.

67

METHOD #2

1. Cut 6 to 7 inches of fabric by the width of the yardage.

2. Make a narrow, rolled hem around the raw edges.

3. Fold lengthwise, right sides together.

4. Leave 12 inches open at either end, but sew the center 12 inches to close the tube.

5. Turn to the right side and press with the seam at the center of the strip, opening the ends.

6. Take a pleat along the center of the ascot to narrow the neckband.

WEARING THE ASCOT

To tie any style of ascot, lay one end over the other and hold the bottom end. Loop the top end under and pull up, behind, then over the top of the lower end. Tighten the half-knot to a comfortable position. Spread the upper flap and even the ends. Secure with a tie-tac, scarf pin or brooch for long-term wearing.

Wear an ascot inside or outside the neckline of a blouse, shirt, jacket, sweater or robe.

When made to be worn exclusively with one specific garment, the center of the ascot can be tacked to the garment at the center back of the neckline, the ends brought around to the front and looped in a half-knot. This keeps it in place when worn .

Theatre Scarf

Slightly larger than the ascot is the theatre scarf. It is a short scarf, usually fringed at the ends. The scarf was originally designed to keep the neck and chest warm and protected when a coat was too much of an encumbrance. It was worn under a short jacket without having the ends show below the hem.

Cut the fabric 12 inches wide by 36 to 40 inches and hem the two long sides. Cut the fabric 24 inches wide and sew it into a tube or double-faced scarf. (See Aviator's Scarf for finishing methods.)

Aviator's Scarf

An aviator's scarf is traditionally a 12-by-60 inch, white silk scarf with fringed ends (see Illus. 62).

Hand-sew a narrow rolled hem along both long sides of a 12-by-60-inch strip of fabric. Silk twist can be looped through the short ends for elegant fringe.

1. For a double-cut, front and facing, you'll need a piece of fabric 24 inches wide by 60 inches long.

Fold along the length, right sides together and sew one long seam. Turn to right side and fold in a narrow seam allowance.

2. Ready-made fringe can be sewn into the hems at each end of the scarf, or you can draw threads from the weave for a self-fringe. A third option for finishing the ends of your scarf is to make your own hand-tied fringe.

HAND-TIED FRINGE

1. Cut silk twist to 14-inch lengths.

2. Use a very small crochet hook to make the tiniest possible hole to pull the fringe through the fabric.

Poke the hook through the fabric at the center of one hem edge from back to front. Fold several strands of silk twist in half and pull the loop through the fabric (Illus. 90).

3. Bring the long ends through the loop and cinch.

Roll the hem while pulling up the loops of the fringe.

4. Work out from the center, in both directions, towards the outer edges. This keeps the fringe even and the fabric flat.

ADDITIONAL NOTES: MORE RECTANGULAR SCARVES

A single 18-by-70-inch silk rectangle is a very dramatic scarf. It can be made from a single strip, hemmed on all four sides. An alternative: Hem the two long sides, self-fringe the remaining ends by pulling cross-threads from the raw edges of the fabric along the short sides.

- Place the center of a long rectangle over your head. Cross the ends in front, under your chin and bring them to the back. Either allow the ends to flow loosely down your back or loop them into a single knot at the nape of your neck. Cover with a broad-brimmed hat for a wonderful touch of glamour (Illus. 91). This will also protect your hair and skin from the harmful rays of the sun.

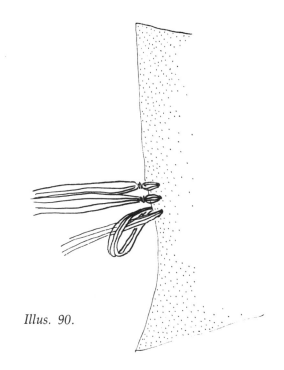

Illus. 90.

- Drape a long rectangle across your throat from front to back. Allow the ends to hang loosely.

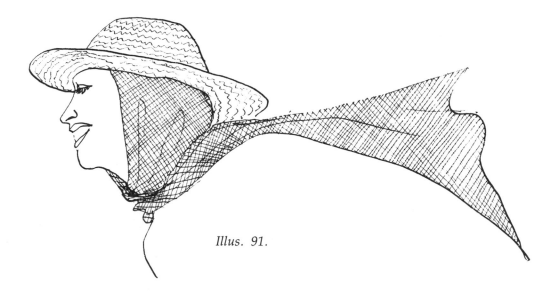

Illus. 91.

Illus. 92.

- Substitute a knotted scarf for that tired string of beads you usually reach for when getting dressed (Illus. 92). The look is fresh and new, the spark of color exciting. A long rectangular scarf of knitted or woven silk, cotton or wool will enhance any costume.

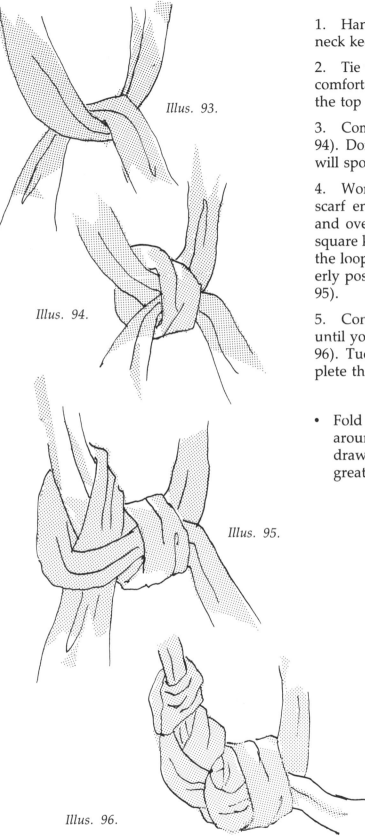

Illus. 93.

Illus. 94.

Illus. 95.

Illus. 96.

1. Hang the scarf around the back of your neck keeping the ends even at the front.

2. Tie the scarf ends into a square knot (at a comfortable height) looping the top end over the top of the knot (Illus. 93).

3. Complete the first or center knot (Illus. 94). Don't cinch the knot too tightly or you will spoil the effect.

4. Working with one end at a time, lead the scarf end under the fabric, around behind, and over the top forming a loop next to the square knot. Slip the end of the scarf through the loop and pull only until the knot is properly positioned next to the center knot (Illus. 95).

5. Continue to wrap a series of single knots until you come to the end of the fabric (Illus. 96). Tuck the ends into the last knot. Complete the other side to match.

• Fold a long rectangle in half, drape it around your neck from back to front, and draw the ends through the loop. This looks great over a bodice with jewel neckline.

- Drape the scarf around your waist from back to front and tie, allowing the two ends to drape over the front of your skirt (Illus. 97).

- Drape a rectangular scarf around the neck from back to front, loop ends at front. To secure, tie ends in a knot and loop one end over the knot. Very nice over a straight sheath.

Illus. 97.

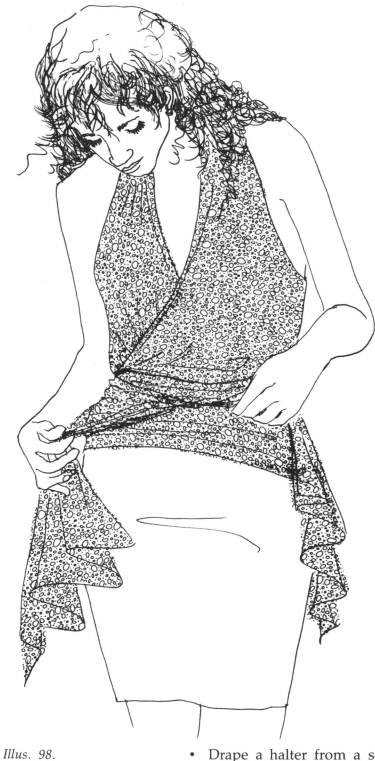

Illus. 98.

• Drape a halter from a square, then tie a matching long scarf around your hipline, over a simple skirt. Secure with a square knot or half-bow (Illus. 98).

- Drape two long scarves from matching or contrasting colors around your hipline. Tie in knots at opposite sides and allow the ends to hang, both sides (Illus. 99).

- Wrap a long rectangle around your neck, under a collar or over a V-neckline. Tie it in a square knot, low on your chest (Illus. 100).

Use these ideas freely; let them inspire some ideas of your own. Make scarves in all imaginable sizes and shapes; they're great for wearing or giving. Follow your whims—and whimsies; it's fun to wear things made from your own original ideas.

Illus. 99.

Illus. 100.

BELTS

A belt is a strip or band of leather (or other material) that is worn around the waist to hold up clothing, define the shape of the body, enhance a costume, or for the sole purpose of supporting tools and other equipment relating to one's occupation. Since this book is dedicated to personal adornment, we will ignore the practical aspect of belts and deal solely with decorative additions.

A belt is a perfect figure enhancer. It can accent a slender waistline, call attention to the rib cage or define the hipline (Illus. 101). Belts can be worn singly or in multiples of your choosing. They add a touch of color to an outfit, convert a simple dress to an evening frock by ringing it with sparkle and glitter or add texture and definition to plain clothing.

NOTES ON WEARING BELTS

Your figure will dictate the type of belt that is best worn about your body. Here are a few tips to help you choose wisely:

Illus. 101.

• **Short and Stocky:** Avoid wide belts that cut you off across the middle of your body. Instead, choose a narrow belt that matches your skirt (Illus. 102). It will define the waistline without making you look shorter and wider. The vertical line of a string of beads is more complimentary to your figure than the horizontal line of an eye-catching belt.

Illus. 102.

• **Tall and Slender:** Your body can accommodate any style of belt, but take advantage of your slenderness to display a wide, colorful belt around your mid-section (Illus. 103). Wear narrow belts in multiples of three or more; try a narrow belt over a wide one to girdle the waist; wrap an obi-type binder with a narrow sash. With your figure, anything goes.

Illus. 103.

• **Long-Waisted** bodies are best suited to wide belts that blend with the skirt of your costume, raising the waistline to a more manageable position. Narrow belts should blend into the color of the lower garment (Illus. 104). Wear them high to define an empire look. Low-wrapped and hipline belts will work if the garment does not define the waistline: a loose-bodied sheath, narrowing around the hipline or a full blouseon that meets the skirt at the hip-bones or below.

Illus. 104.

- **Short-waisted** bodies do well in hip-belts or belts that match the blouse and elongate the upper torso. A loosely wrapped belt to define an empire look only if you have a small bosom; a belt with bottom-edge definition to make the waistline seem a little lower (Illus. 105).

- **Broad hips** look even wider when you cinch a belt too tight (Illus. 106). Wear it a little on the loose side to even up your silhouette. Choose a narrow belt that will blend into your clothing.

All this points up the fact that there is an endless list of possibilities for making belts. Start from the simplest forms of waistline enhancers and let your imagination run free.

Illus. 106.

Illus. 105.

Ultrasuede Belts

The wonderful part about making an Ultrasuede belt is that when the fabric is cut and trimmed, the belt is ready to wear. Ultrasuede is a man-made fabric that does not fray or ravel. It needs no reinforcing, retains its quality appearance through repeated washings and extensive wear. It comes in a huge assortment of colors, a selection of prints and patterns, and is commonly available in 45-to-60-inch widths.

Ultrasuede is a rather expensive fabric but don't let that scare you; it can be purchased by the inch. This cuts the finished cost of each belt, considerably. Purchase only the amount of fabric you actually need, with Ultrasuede there's never any waste.

REQUIREMENTS

Buy 3 to 5 inches of Ultrasuede in a color of your choice and you have almost completed your belt.

DIRECTIONS

1. Trim the ends to a point on each side (Illus. 107).

2. Wrap smooth and flat or scrunch the material to a preferred width; Tie in a knot to wear (Illus. 108).

This is the simplest form of belt. The immediate results make it a fun accessory. Now, the next step. The following suggestions are still tie belts, but with some fancy additions.

Start with the same amount of Ultrasuede that you bought for the first belt.

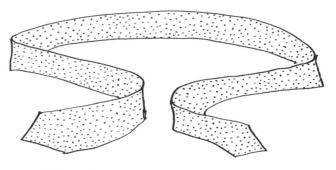

Illus. 107.

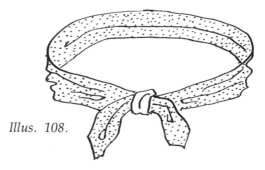

Illus. 108.

1. Trim both ends of the fabric to points. Sew completely around the entire belt with matching or contrasting thread, ¼ inch from the cut edge (Illus. 109). Use either a straight stitch or an embroidery cam for a decorative finish.

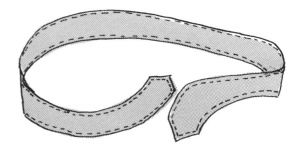

Illus. 109.

2. Buy two lengths of Ultrasuede in contrasting colors or patterns. Place the two pieces of fabric together, back to back. Topstitch around the outside, ¼ inch from the edge (Illus. 110). This gives you a totally versatile, reversible belt to perk up many different outfits.

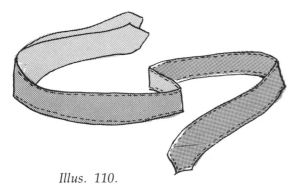

Illus. 110.

3. Trim one end of the belting to a point. Attach D-rings to the opposite end (Illus. 111). Sew as close to the rings as possible using the zipper foot on your conventional machine. Your belt is ready to wear.

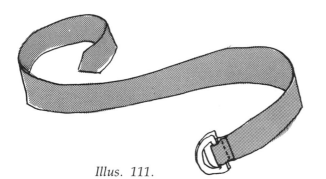

Illus. 111.

Assorted Belts with Buckles

Use buckles singly or in multiples of two or more. Make them a decorative accent; They don't have to be purely practical. There are several basic styles of buckle from which to choose.

• The first is a simple buckle with a center post (Illus. 112). The square end of the belt is wrapped around the post and stitched in place. The shaped end of the belt is threaded through the buckle and held in place by friction.

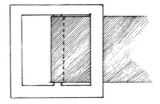

Illus. 112.

• The second style of buckle is one with a movable prong attached to a center post (Illus. 113). Punch a hole through the square end of the belt to admit the prong, wrap the end of the strap around the post

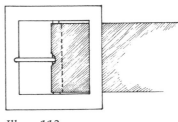

Illus. 113.

and stitch. Punch three to five holes through the opposite end of the strap to admit the prong and hold the belt at a desired point. The assortment of holes (or eyelets) provides size adjustment.

- The third style of buckle has a stationary prong or hook on the back that has much the same effect as the movable tongue-type prong of the second style of buckle (Illus. 114). It, too, hooks through a hole or eye in the end of the strap or belt. This style of buckle is usually highly decorated and is common to the Western-style belt. It has a bracket or bar on the back for attaching the belt. Insert two grip fasteners through the square end of the strap and snap the end over the bracket. The buckle may be transferred to other belts.

- There is also an interlocking buckle that comes in two styles: the first works on the same principle as the hook and eye, the second works with a magnetic clasp (Illus. 115). These buckles are commonly used with elastic or woven webbing for sportswear.

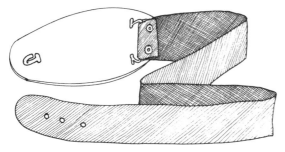

Illus. 114.

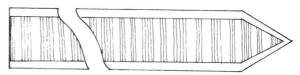

Illus. 115.

Any type of fabric can be sewn to a buckle. Woven or knitted fabrics are usually too stretchy or flimsy to be used without some type of reinforcement and should be interfaced. Leather, natural or synthetic, can be attached to a buckle with no additional stiffening or support.

A reinforced inner-webbing called belting is available by the yard or in small packages at most fabric shops. (Directions for use are included with each package.) Belting is an interfacing designed specifically to add substance to lightweight fabrics when used for making self-belts. Medium to heavyweight fabrics only need some interfacing (common, non-woven interfacing) to be firm enough for practical use.

GENERAL DIRECTIONS

1. Cut the belting to the measurement of your waist plus 3-to-5 inches for overlap. Leave one end square, the other is pointed (Illus. 116).

Illus. 116.

2. Measure the fabric cover for your belt: (Illus. 117)

Illus. 117.

Length = the length of the interfacing plus ¼-inch seam allowance for the pointed end;

Width = the width of the belting plus ¼-inch seam allowance each side or ½-inch.

3. Pin the strip of fabric to the belting. Overlap the edges on the long sides and mitre the fabric at the corners or points (Illus. 118).

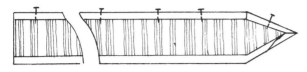

Illus. 118.

4. Cut the backing:

Leather or synthetic leather needs no seam allowance.

Fabric requires a turned edge to prevent fraying (¼ inch, all around).

5. Pin the belt backing in place around three sides leaving the square end with the raw fabric sticking out, the opposite or pointed end fully enclosed.

Topstitch the three layers together (Illus. 119).

Illus. 119.

6. Punch a hole through the square end of the belt, large enough to admit the buckle prong (Illus. 120).

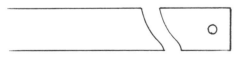

Illus. 120.

7. Fold the square end of the belt over the buckle post and stitch the buckle in place, using a zipper foot to sew as close to the post as possible (Illus. 121).

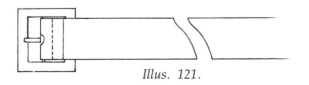

Illus. 121.

8. Punch holes at the opposite end of the belt and reinforce with metal eyelets to preserve the fabric (Illus. 122).

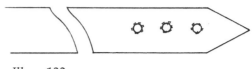

Illus. 122.

Double-Wrapped Belts

1. Make two separate buckled belts with a tab at the center back to hold them together. These belts can either be the same or a different width (Illus. 123).

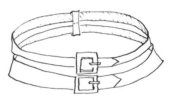

Illus. 123.

2. A wide back with two separate straps at the front (Illus. 124). May be as wide as 2 to 3 inches at the back, tapering to two ¾-inch tabs at the front.

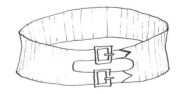

Illus. 124.

3. A double length, 1-inch-wide belt that wraps twice around the waist and/or hips with the end looped through the buckle. Wear it with the closure off-center at the front (Illus. 125). This one: 2½ to 3 times your waist measurement.

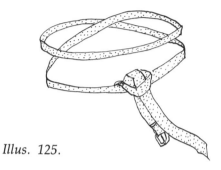

Illus. 125.

4. Wear an obi-style belt with the wide portion starting at the front and crossing in back, and the ends tapering to a narrow front closure. Make it from satin or brocade with a rhinestone buckle—a very dressy transformation for simple separates (Illus. 126).

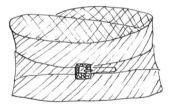

Illus. 126.

Embroidered Belts

Machine- or hand-embroider the fabric for your belt (Illus. 127). Add a commercial buckle, D-rings or a closure of your creation and you have a unique belt, a true one-of-a-kind.

Illus. 127.

84

SUGGESTED FABRIC, NOTIONS, ETC.

Any woven or knitted fabric, leather, suede or synthetic, plain or print.

Interfacing and backing for woven or knit fabrics.

Thread: silky machine embroidery cones or hand-embroidery floss.

Hoops suitable to machine- or hand-embroidery.

DIRECTIONS

Machine-embroidery is best done before the fabric is cut. Allow approximately 1½ inches all the way around the design for seam allowance and shrinkage. Hand-embroidering draws up the fabric a little, machine-embroidery might draw it up a lot. You wouldn't want the finished piece to be too small after putting in all that effort.

Plan the design to suit the shape and size of the belt. Back wovens and knits with interfacing before starting the embroidery. Stretch fabric in a hoop whether you are working by hand or machine. The tension of hand-embroidery is easier to control than that of machine work, but it's wise to protect the shape of the belt.

If you are embroidering on leather (natural or synthetic), make the stitches a little on the loose side and keep the back as neat as possible. Leather won't need any interfacing as it is firm enough to retain its shape. At most you'll want a light protection for the back of the stitching, such as thin lining leather or light-weight fabric.

Start at the center of the design and work out towards the ends. This prevents buckling in the middle of the design.

Embroider the design within the planned shape. Sew the fabric to the interfacing and then cut the excess fabric to within ¼ inch of the contour of the belt. Complete the backing and attach the buckle.

Rope Belts

The drapery department of your local fabric shop is the place to find "silk" rope commonly used as tiebacks for drapery panels. This twisted cord is purchased by the yard, off huge spools. Trim with large wooden beads, decorative tassels or anything else you might choose (Illus. 128). Occasionally, this type of rope can be found ready-to-wear; precut to the appropriate lengths, already trimmed with matching tassels at both ends.

Choose several lengths of cord (it is usually made of rayon threads), wind, braid, twist or otherwise put them together in matching or contrasting colors.

Combine a variety of cords in assorted yarns and textures such as natural hemp, sisal or fabric sewn into long tubes. Macramé cord has a fine texture and is available in a wide variety of weights and colors.

Illus. 128.

Knot the ends of the cord leaving an inch or two hanging below the knot. Separate the threads of each strand to make fluffy tassels. Intersperse the strands with beads or shell for a change of texture.

Cabbage Rose Belt

This is a very sophisticated accessory. A simple dress becomes an elegant gown with the addition of this beautiful belt (Illus. 129).

DESCRIPTION

The belt is made from three strips of voile sewn into tubes and braided. One to three fabric roses (see Fabric Flowers, page 124) and several leaves (see Leaf Collar, page 131 for directions) are sewn over the top end of the fabric. Velcro tape is used for the closure.

SUGGESTED FABRIC

Nylon voile or other sheer, firmly woven fabric. Can be made from fabric to match any garment.

REQUIREMENTS

Approximately 1 yard of sheer fabric.
⅔ yard matching ribbon
2 inches of Velcro tape
Matching thread

Yardage requirements can vary with texture and width of the fabric.

Illus. 129.

DIRECTIONS

Cut three strips of fabric, width: 3 to 4 inches, length: your waist measurement plus approximately 5 inches. Loosely braiding the fabric takes up a great deal of the slack; don't come up short.

1.   Fold each strip in half lengthwise, wrong side out. Sew across one short end and down the long side on an overlock machine. Turn fabric to right side. Finish remaining strips to match.

2.   Twist the three strips together into a loose braid, approximately 2 inches wide. Conceal the seams at the center of each strip as you make the braid (Illus. 130).

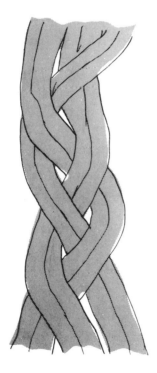

Illus. 130.

3.   Double-fold the raw ends of each tube to the wrong side of the braid and sew flat on a conventional sewing machine (Illus. 131). This forms a firm base for attaching the flowers and leaves.

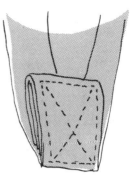

Illus. 131.

4.   Pin ¼-to-½-inch ribbon down the center back of braid. Fold one raw end under and space the ribbon along the braid without pulling the twists (Illus. 132). The ribbon reinforces the plaits and prevents the braid from losing its shape.

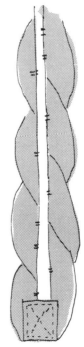

Illus. 132.

5. Tack the ribbon in place (down the center of the braid) keeping the length to your waistline measurement plus 3 inches for overlap.

6. Machine-sew the Velcro tape to ends.

Use one to three large cabbage roses and three leaves to complete this beautiful accessory. Pin the leaves and roses to the belt at the reinforced end. Put the belt around your waist to adjust the positioning of the flowers to your satisfaction, then sew securely to the belt.

This is not only an exotic accessory for your own use; it makes a most coveted gift.

Elastic Belts

Elastic webbing makes an excellent sport belt. It breathes with you and never restricts your movements.

- Cut the elastic to the measurement of your waistline. Wrap ½ to ¾ inch of elastic around the posts of an interlocking or magnetic buckle and machine-stitch, using a zipper foot (Illus. 133).

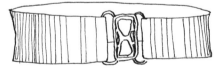

Illus. 133.

- Make elastic belts with leather closures (Illus. 134). The elastic is measured approximately 2 inches less than your actual waistline measurement to prevent the belt from overlapping.

Cut the leather tabs double to hide the ends of the elastic. Place one tab under, one over each end of the elastic and top-stitch through the three thicknesses.

Punch holes through the ends and lace with a thong.

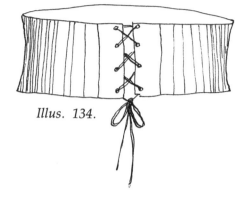

Illus. 134.

- Cover 1½- or 2-inch waistband elastic with fabric to match a skirt or dress (Illus. 135). Cut the elastic 2 inches less than your waistline measurement. The length of the fabric is 1½ times your waist measurement, the width is twice the width of the elastic plus ½-inch seam allowance. You'll also need an interlocking or magnetic buckle.

Sew the fabric into a tube with right sides together. Reverse the tube and slide the elastic inside, centering the seam down the length. Sew one part of the buckle to each end and even the fabric by stretching the belt to its full length.

Illus. 135.

- Sew an elastic peplum belt (Illus. 136). Use 2-to-3-inch-wide elastic for this waist-minimizer. You'll need about 2 inches less than your waistline measurement.

Illus. 136.

The ruffle for the bottom edge is 3-inch-wide nylon lace, approximately 1½ times your hip measurement.

Fashion one medium-size rose or three small ribbon roses for the closure or use a rhinestone buckle.

Bind the ends of the elastic with velvet or satin ribbon.

Pin the lace to the elastic, evenly spaced along the entire length. Stretch the elastic to the spacing of the lace as you sew, using a long, loose zigzag stitch.

Attach three fur hooks and eyes to the front closure, add the fabric flowers, and your belt is ready to wear.

Flounces, Peplums, and Overskirts

Get an invitation to a fancy party, a banquet, or a ball and the first thought to cross your mind is, "What shall I wear?"

Evening wear traditionally means extra clothing: shoes, dresses, lingerie and other items of wearing apparel that are reserved for special occasions only. Today, fashion takes a simpler turn. There is no longer a reason for anyone to have a warehouse full of rarely worn clothing when a selection of basics can be dressed-up for special occasions.

An overskirt is one of the most wonderful wardrobe extenders you can sew; the soft flow of fabric always seems to bring with it a fairy tale princess feeling. Tie an overskirt over a simple dress and you know you're dressed to go to the ball.

Cut in assorted styles and lengths, overskirts create a new and exciting look for a multitude of everyday garments. A tailored dress or that simple knit top and straight skirt that takes you to the office will also take you to the theater, a cocktail party or an evening of dancing with the addition of a flounce, peplum or overskirt (Illus. 137).

The style and length of an overskirt is limited only by your personal taste and preference. An effective overskirt can be as simple as a gathered length of tulle or net hung from a grosgrain ribbon. Wrap a silk flounce around your hips and your office dress is fashionable enough for elegant late-day-into-evening wear. Your overskirt can also be more detailed—like a flamenco skirt.

Illus. 137.

A LITTLE ABOUT FABRIC CHOICES

Create the most usable overskirts in colors that work with your basic clothing. A strong textural difference between the overskirt and the garment it covers adds a touch of excitement for evening. Medium-weight taffeta over tweed, satin over knits or crepe—shiny over matte, texture over slick—each combination provides the maximum contrast. For subtle effects, match your overskirts to specific garments.

Separate peplums can be made from any type of fabric: silk, crepe de chine, tulle, chiffon or ottoman. Each fabric results in a different effect. The *style* of overskirt you choose usually dictates whether the fabric should be soft and draped or firm and substantial.

Lace is another attractive addition to one's wardrobe. It is available in a variety of forms: edgings to border other fabrics, yardage with or without self-edgings, one solid color, a solid color combined with metallic threads or woven entirely from metallic threads. This gives you the opportunity to use lace for an entire overskirt or combine with other fabrics. Each fabric or combination means an entirely new and different feel for a basic dress.

All of the overskirts illustrated in this chapter are based on a few easy styles detailed in the general directions. The important changes are personal ones: The length of each style you sew, and the amount of fullness you add.

SELECT A SUITABLE LENGTH

The most flattering length for an overskirt is one of your own choosing. Only you can tell which lines will best suit your figure. Finding the best lengths for overskirts is similar to choosing a skirt length.

Stand in front of a mirror with a piece of fabric wide enough to cover an area from your waist to the floor. Tuck one long side of the fabric under your belt to secure it. Not wearing a belt? Use a safety pin to hold a length of 1-inch elastic around your waistline and keep the fabric in place. Readjust the length of the fabric by gathering it into your hands and tucking it into the waist-stay. Each time you find a flattering placement, write down the measurement. Those are the lengths you want for your peplum and/or overskirts.

GENERAL INFORMATION

Overskirt is a term that includes any skirt that is worn over another garment: Sheers that are too revealing to be worn alone; open skirts that would expose too much of the body to view without another garment underneath; any skirt that doesn't work on its own. The lengths for overskirts range from approximately hipbone to the floor.

Flounce and peplum are familiar terms within the range of overskirts. The difference between them is that a flounce is a wide ruffle that can be placed almost anywhere while a peplum starts at the waist or upper hipline and rarely falls below the break of the upper thigh. Common usage has made these terms almost interchangeable.

Hemlines for overskirts can be cut straight across, graded from one side to the other or front to back, scalloped, ruffled or anything else you can dream up to add to the list. In other words, the only limits involved in finishing overskirts are the limits of your own imagination.

HEMLINES AND FINISHES

Vary the hemline of a peplum of overskirt. There are many styles from which to choose.

- **Scallops:** Plan the size and shape for each curve. Make a template, a firm pattern cut from tagboard or heavy plastic that will withstand repeated tracing and not bend or tear. To be sure that each arc is the same size and properly spaced, trace the pattern along a designated line (Illus. 138).

- **Asymmetric:** A sharply graded hemline, short at one point, dropping long on the opposite side (Illus. 139). This style (the asymmetric hemline) makes for the graceful flow of fabric whether it is cut circular, straight or on the bias. Mark your chosen length for the front and the back and gently curve the hemline between the two measurements.

- **Bubble:** Cut fabric either on the straight of the grain or on the bias. Dart or pleat around the waist to meet the measurement of the waistband. Then dart the fabric around the hemline with half the number of darts used across the top of the skirt. The overskirt will stand out around the hipline and curve back towards the body along the lower edge (Illus. 140).

MORE ABOUT HEMLINES

- Use the unhemmed edge of net or choose border-edged lace for the final finish of your overskirt or peplum. These are fabrics that won't ravel. You only have to take a sharp scissor and clean-cut the edge of net or tulle, follow the pattern or design around the outside edge of the lace for a usable finish on fabric of this type.

- Sew lace edging, velvet, grosgrain or embroidered ribbon completely around the outside edges (Illus. 141). Use a narrow zigzag stitch on your conventional sewing machine to attach the edging.

- Make a 3- or 4-inch ruffle to go completely around the outside of the overskirt. a) *Single Ruffle:* Hem one edge of a strip of fabric and gather along the opposite long side. b) *Double Ruffle:* Hem both sides of the fabric strip (on an overlock machine) and gather the ruffle at the center rather than along one edge (Illus. 142).

- Create your own edge binding by cutting narrow bias strips from fabric that matches or contrasts with a specific dress.

Illus. 138.   Illus. 139.   Illus. 140.   Illus. 141.   Illus. 142.

WAISTLINE DETAILS

Circle-Cut Fabric: The upper edge of the skirt is eased into the band.

Straight-Cut Fabric: The skirt is either gathered to the waistband or darted to fit the designated space.

To gather the waistline of the skirt: Sew a long basting stitch across the top edge. Draw up the thread until the waistline fits the marked space of the band.

Darted Waistline: Mark the skirt along the top edge for the number of darts needed to bring the waist in to the proper measurement (waist size minus approximately 2 to 3 inches). Sew darts and try the skirt before finishing the waistband. Be sure there is enough gap at the front to tie the band into a bow without drawing in the fabric from the skirt.

Overskirts can be laid out on the yardage in any direction that is suitable to the design and/or weave of the fabric: with the straight of the grain, on the bias, or as a circle. Each layout will give a different effect.

1. Cut with the straight of the grain, lengthwise or cross-grain, for poufed, dirndl-type gathering (Illus. 143).

2. Cut on the true bias for subtle gathering around the hips with graceful fullness spreading to the hemline (Illus. 144).

3. Cut the overskirt from a circle pattern and you have an almost all-bias garment that falls softly over the hipline and swings loose and easy around the hem (Illus. 145).

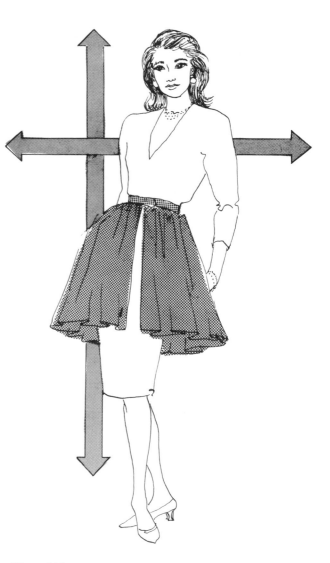

Illus. 143.

Peplum: Straight Cut

The simplest form of peplum is a hip-length skirt, similar to a dancer's tutu, that hangs from a grosgrain or velvet waistband. You won't need a separate pattern for this simple overskirt. Just cut the fabric across the grain or with it, directly from the following dimensions:

Waistband: a) Cut a sash-style waistband along the selvage. Use your waistline measurement, plus enough length for a generous bow by a width of 4 inches. b) Choose grosgrain or velvet ribbon of adequate length to go around the waistline and tie in a bow.

Skirt Width: 1½ to 2 times your hipline measurement.

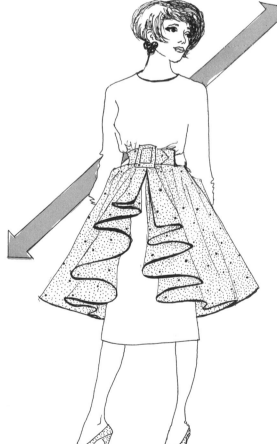

Illus. 144.

Illus. 145.

Length: your chosen length, plus seam and hem allowance (where necessary).

Check your hipline measurement before you buy the fabric; the length and width for the finished overskirt determines the amount of fabric you need for your peplum.

Rule-of-Thumb: *The longer the hemline, the fuller the overskirt.* A longer hemline is more graceful with additional width. Don't be afraid of wearing too much material. Fullness can be controlled along the upper edge with pleats or darts; the bottom portion remains luxuriously full.

Peplum: Circle Cut

A circular peplum is almost a total bias garment. It is lovely when made from a softly flowing fabric such as silk Charmeuse, satin, shiny rayon, lightweight taffetas or a soft crepe. The waistline is eased or gathered into a buttoned, snapped or tied waistband.

- With narrow-width fabrics you need at least two lengths. Yardage widths of 36 or 45 inches will not gather around the hips; they're much too skimpy. Plan a single seam at the center back or evenly space two side-seams.

- Most peplum styles can be cut from one length of 54-to-60-inch fabric. Grosgrain or velvet ribbon is then substituted for the self-band as you will probably want the entire width of the material for the skirt.

- Use extra-wide fabric (anything over 60 inches) and you can cut a generous overskirt plus the waistband from a single length.

CONSTRUCTION DETAILS

1. French-seam the panels or bind the seam edges. A neat finish is important where the seams might be visible.

2. Complete the hem around three sides.

3. Run a long gathering stitch along the fourth side.

4. Mark the sash for the center on the cut edge.

Measure and mark evenly across the center point your waistline measurement minus 2½ inches.

5. Pin the center back of the skirt to the center point of the waistband; pin the edges to the outer marks. Pull up the gathering thread to fit within the marked points.

6. Stitch the waistband to the skirt. Press.

DIRECTIONS

When you cut a circular style for your peplum, you can increase the size of the waistline by adding a few inches to the radius of the upper line. This will provide additional width for the gathering around the top of the peplum.

The dimensions for the peplum are:

Waistline: Radius—⅓ your actual hipline measurement (plus whatever extra width you desire: at least 2 to 3 inches).

Hemline: The chosen length for the peplum, plus a seam allowance for the waistline (¼ to ½ inch), plus the hem allowance (½ to 1 inch).

1. Fold the fabric across the grain to equal the total length for the peplum plus the radius for the waistline.

2. Draw the waistline: Secure the end of a tape measure in the folded corner. Stretch the tape to the measurement of the waistline. Move the tape around the apex and draw a series of marks below the bottom to the tape measure. Use a piece of tailor's chalk, a sliver of soap or insert pins through the fabric at short intervals around the line (Illus. 146).

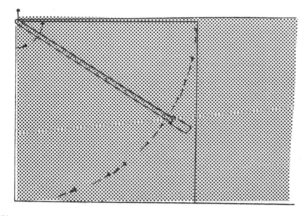

Illus. 146.

3. Mark the hem: Do not move the tape from its anchor point. Stretch the tape to the hem length by measuring from the line of the waist to where you want your hem. (Add the waist and length measurement together to find the lower cutting edge.) Mark as above.

4. Cut a straight waistband long enough to accommodate your style choice: tied or lapped. a) *Waist Wrap:* Your waist measurement plus 2½ inches for overlap. b) *Tie:* Your waist measurement plus ample length to tie in a bow.

5. Cut the peplum along the marked lines. Sew the hem completely around the skirt. Pin the waistband to the skirt. Gather the fabric to fit between the marked points and sew.

Peplum: Asymmetric Hemline

The asymmetric peplum shows the most graceful flow of fabric (Illus. 147). When cut on the bias or as a circle, the gathers fall softly, all around. It can be worn with the short portion of the skirt at the front, back, or either side; attractive in any direction. This style can also be cut from the straight of the fabric.

Illus. 147.

Make the asymmetric style from heavy or stiff fabrics such as taffeta, ottoman, moiré, brocade or other highly decorative yardage and you will find it most effective when not too fully gathered around the waist. A darted or pleated waistline shows off heavy fabric to better advantage. Leave the full, tight gathers for sheers and draped material such as China silk, chiffon, tulle or net and soft lace.

DIRECTIONS:

The first directions are for an overskirt with an asymmetric hemline, cut on the straight grain of the fabric.

Determine the length of the shortest portion of the skirt (the front opening) and longest portion of the skirt (the center back).

1. Fold the fabric in half, matching selvages.

2. Mark the long length of the back along the fold of the fabric, the short length of the front at the open (selvage) side (Illus. 148). Grade the hemline between the two marks leaving approximately 6 to 10 inches straight across the fabric at the center back.

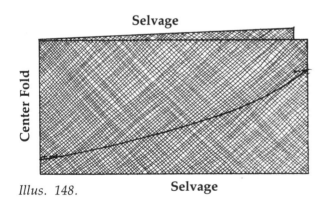

Illus. 148.

3. Follow the finishing directions given for Straight-Cut Peplum. (Darts or pleats around the waistline for heavy fabric, gathers for softer material.)

98

Peplum: Circular Asymmetric

Follow the same general directions whether you are drafting a pattern or cutting the overskirt directly from the fabric, making a short peplum or floor-length skirt. Only the length changes; not the directions.

1. Secure the tape measure to the folded corner of the fabric (or indicate the fold line on the pattern).

2. Stretch the tape to the waist measurement (⅓ your actual waistline measurement plus 3 inches for fullness). Draw the waistline of the pattern.

3. Move the end of the tape measure from the upper point of the fold to the juncture of the fold and the waistline just drawn (Illus. 149). Stretch the tape to the length you have chosen for the back of the skirt and draw the line for the hem.

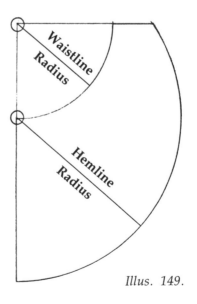

Illus. 149.

WAISTBAND

Mark the waistband for center back and center front. Allow at least 3 inches between the front edges of the skirt or set the edges as far apart as the width of your hipbones if the waistband is to be tied into a bow or knot. This provides the room to tie the band without pulling the fabric of the skirt into the bow.

The edges of the skirt can meet at the center if you are using an overlapped waistband. Your peplum can be worn with the opening at the front, back, or turned to the side for a varied effect.

Mark the band for center back and your waistline measurement, minus 3 inches. Gather or dart the waistline of the skirt to the measurement indicated between the marks.

LONGER-LENGTH OVERSKIRTS

Cut full-length overskirts from the same assortment of fabrics you might choose for a peplum.

Full-length overskirts can be fashioned to meet a daytime dress hemline, hang above it, or barely graze the floor (Illus. 150). The length of the dress underneath does not affect the length of the overskirt.

A mid-thigh or knee-length overskirt could be used for late afternoon dressing; mid-calf to floor-length is for glamorous occasions, such as dancing and formal parties. With a knee-length dress, a long overskirt is flirty (Illus. 151).

Curve the bottom-front points to blend nicely from the edges into the lower hem. For a floor-length overskirt, start the curve slightly above the knee area.

Illus. 150.

99

Illus. 151.

Tiered Overskirts

Making a tiered overskirt is much easier than the finished product would indicate (Illus. 152). Sew the entire peplum or overskirt from bias or circular-cut fabric.

Extend the length of the first tier from the waistline to the top of the thigh (approximately 10 to 12 inches). Cut the second or undertier equal to the measurement from the waistline to a point halfway between the bottom of the first tier and the hem of your skirt (16 to 20 inches).

DIRECTIONS: BIAS-CUT

1. Find the true bias of your fabric. Measure and mark the tiers along the bias line.

2. Cut and piece tiers where necessary to achieve the desired width.

DIRECTIONS: CIRCLE-CUT

See directions for Peplum: Circle Cut for complete information on cutting a circular overskirt. Each tier is cut as a separate skirt, a half-circle.

FINISHING TIERED SKIRT

To make the fabric lie a little closer to the body, gather both tiers together on a single or double thread. For puffy layers, gather each tier separately, and to exaggerate the fluffiness of the tiers, underline each row, along the waistline, with a 3-to-4-inch-wide strip of nylon net or tulle.

Bias-Cut: Use the slanting ends of each row for the hem-edge at the fronts. Round the points at the bottom-front edges of each tier for easier hemming.

Illus. 152.

Flamenco-Style Overskirt

A single ruffle is a fun trim for an overskirt. It can easily be added to any of the designs for a little extra zing, but there is nothing that makes you feel quite as saucy as the multi-tiered, ruffled style of the flamenco skirt (Illus. 153). The exaggerated rows of gathered fabric seem to put extra snap into your dancing feet. Sew this very feminine overskirt for the fun of it.

Illus. 153.

The entire skirt is made in three rows or tiers; each tier is gathered separately, then stitched to the row above. The center front of the skirt ends at the top of the thigh approximately 9 inches of the total length. The center back hangs to the floor—a total length of 42 inches.

Make a pattern for this skirt. It's an exciting style that you'll probably want to repeat. Duplicate the first overskirt in another fabric or even try some variations of the design. The pattern gives you a place to start a new version without having to remeasure the entire garment.

The information detailed below is for an overskirt, 9 inches long at the front, dropping to 42 inches at the back. The width will accommodate a hipline measurement to approximately 42 to 43 inches. The tiers are cut on the lengthwise grain of the fabric for seamless construction.

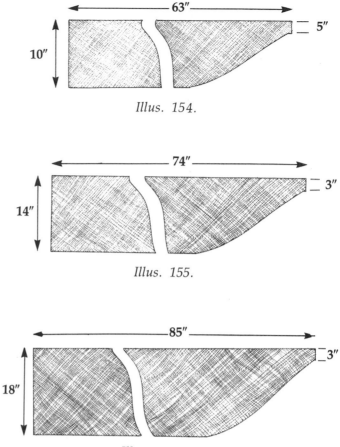

Illus. 154.

Illus. 155.

Illus. 156.

DRAFTING THE PATTERN

1. The top tier, the narrowest one, is approximately 3 inches deep at the front and grades to 10 inches at the center back. Use a hem curve to draw the lower lines of the tiers. Keep the first 4 inches of the front and the center back 12 inches of the hemline straight. Curve slightly between these points.

The width of the top strip is 1½ times your hip measurement (approximately 63 inches) to allow for the gathers (Illus. 154).

2. The second tier, like the first, starts at a depth of 3 inches at the center front. It is graded to hang 14 inches below the first tier at the center back. The first 5 inches of the front and the center 14 inches of the back hemline is drawn straight across, the remaining portion of the hemline is curved to fit between these points.

The width of the second tier is approximately 74 inches or 1¾ times your hipline measurement (Illus. 155).

3. The third tier is also cut 3 inches long at the center front. The center-back hemline curves to a depth of 18 inches. Keep the first 6 inches of the hemline and the center back 16 inches straight across.

The width of the third tier is approximately 84 inches, or twice your hipline measurement (Illus. 156).

As you can see from these measurements, each succeeding tier is cut a little longer and a little wider than the preceding one. This gives the skirt a nice sweep towards the back as you walk or dance. It is a glamorous overskirt with an elegant feel.

The details given for this pattern are for cutting the skirt on the lengthwise grain of the fabric. The flamenco overskirt requires approximately 2½ yards of 45-inch fabric.

103

If you prefer to cut the finished pattern on the cross-grain or on the bias, plan to add seams equally, at the sides of each tier or at the center back. Example: If the fabric is 45 inches wide and you are cutting the third tier of approximately 84 inches, you must plan a center-back seam (two segments of 42 inches = 84 inches) plus the seam allowance. It can also be cut with side seams: the full back plus two side panels to complete the width. However you divide the pattern, be sure to keep both sides even and don't forget the seam allowance for each additional segment you create.

If the seam allowance is all that prevents the pattern from fitting on the fabric (in one piece), hedge a little. Use ¼-inch seams and roll a narrow hem around the outside.

WAISTBAND

Cut the waistband sash 4 to 6 inches wide by 60 to 70 inches long. Mark the center and evenly space your waistline measurement minus 3 inches across the center mark.

Topstitch a narrow rolled hem around both ends of the waistband outside the portion that is sewn to the skirt.

FINISHING THE SKIRT

1. Run a gathering thread across the top of each tier. Pin the first row to the waistband, between the marks, and draw up the thread to fit the space. Stitch in place.

2. Pin the next ruffle to the preceding one and gather to fit the hem of the first tier. Sew in place.

3. Pin, gather, and sew the third ruffle to the bottom of the second tier. Fold the waistband over the top of the skirt and topstitch the center portion, leaving the ends open to form a large bow when worn.

You do have the option of either sewing a conventional hem all the way around the skirt or adding a ruffle for the finished edge. If you opt for the ruffle, be sure to try on the skirt to check the length. You might have to shorten it an inch or two before adding the finishing ruffle.

RUFFLE

Measure the outside edge, all the way around the skirt. Cut enough 3-inch wide strips of fabric to equal a length twice the measurement around the outside of the skirt. Sew the strips together, forming one long piece of fabric. Either topstitch a rolled hem down both sides of the fabric strip or run the entire piece through the overlock machine to complete a hem all the way around the outside.

Sew a gathering thread down the center of the fabric strip (Illus. 157). Quarter the strip and insert a pin at each point. Quarter the hem of the overskirt and pin the ruffle in place matching the folded points of the hemline and the pins in the ruffle. Draw up the gathering thread. Sew the ruffle to the skirt.

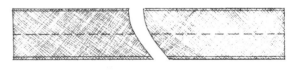

Illus. 157.

A good way to utilize the fabric left after you've finished your overskirt is to make a matching cabbage rose (see page 124). It can be worn over the knot at the front of the skirt or pinned to the shoulder of your bodice for an additional decorative note.

Pocket Peplum

Suspend oversize pockets of crepe-backed satin or rich brocade from a cummerbund for a look of tailored elegance (Illus. 158). This accessory will enhance a straight or A-line garment, a jumpsuit or top with matching pants.

A pocket peplum takes a mere ⅓ yard: 12 inches of 45-inch-wide fabric. You will also need 1 yard of 3-inch-wide grosgrain ribbon to back the waistband.

Illus. 158.

STYLE #1 (Illus. 159)

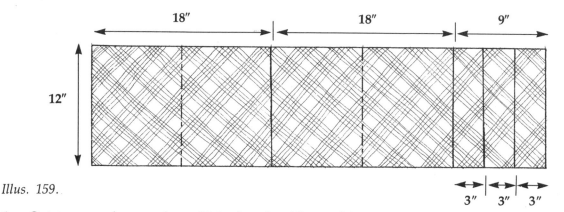

Illus. 159.

1. Cut two pocket sections 12 inches by 18 inches. These measurements can vary to suit your figure. Choose a size for the pockets that is in proportion to your height and girth.

2. Fold the pocket, match the 12-inch ends, right sides together.

Sew the first 2 inches of the seam, leave the next 6 inches open, then complete the bottom 4 inches of the seam. Reinforce the beginning and end of each line of stitching.

3. Leave the top edge open. Stitch across the bottom edge of the pocket, turn the fabric to the right side and press.

Complete the other pocket to match the first. Just be sure you create a left and right pocket segment.

4. Cut the remaining 9-by-12-inch strip of fabric into three equal portions for the waistband, each 3 inches wide by 12 inches long.

Sew the short ends together forming a strip 3 inches wide by 36 inches long. Interface the strip. Sew the ribbon to the band across the top edge.

5. Along the lower edge of the waistband, locate and mark the points on each side that will meet your side seams. Position the pocket openings 1 inch behind these marks and pin them in place. Be sure the openings are facing out, away from the center of the peplum. The waistband has a center-front closure.

Ease the pocket tops gently as you sew the raw edges to the waistband.

6. Topstitch the facing on the inside of the waistband to cover the raw edges at the top of each pocket.

STYLE #2 (Illus. 160)

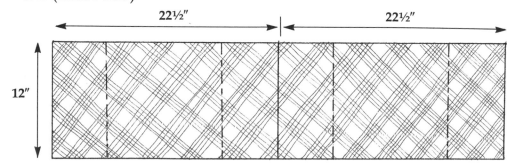

Illus. 160.

You can cut more copious pockets for the peplum and still get the peplum out of ⅓ yard of 45-inch material.

This style calls for pockets that use the entire width of the fabric. The waistband is cut from either grosgrain or velvet ribbon.

1. Cut the fabric in half: two segments, 12 inches by 22½ inches.

2. Fold each segment down the middle and stitch a seam along the 12-inch side as follows: Sew 2 inches, skip the next 6 inches, then sew to the bottom of the fabric. Refold the pocket with the seam at the center of the piece and sew across the bottom edge.

3. There are two options for the waistband: a) Cut a double length of ribbon (outside and facing) to go around your waist and tie into a bow or b) Cut the ribbon to the measurement of your waistline with enough length for the ends to overlap.

A strip of grosgrain or velvet ribbon approximately 2½ yards long is about the average length for the bow-tied waistband; the measurement of your waistline, plus 2 inches for overlap is right for a band with a simple overlapped closure.

Sew the pockets to the waistband with the openings approximately 1 inch forward of the side-seam point.

For an overlapped closure: Attach a snap, hook and eye, grip fastener, Velcro tape or button and buttonhole at the ends. Any of these closures are completely satisfactory.

STYLE #3 (Illus. 161)

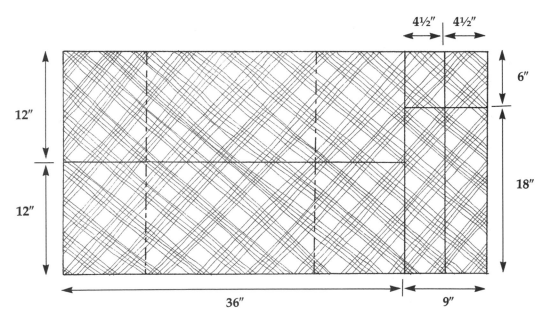

Illus. 161.

This pocket peplum has very large pockets that wrap completely around each hip and almost meet at the center front and center back. A cummerbund waistband completes the peplum nicely. The entire overskirt uses ⅔ yard of 45-inch fabric.

1. *Waistband:* Along the selvage (at one side) cut a strip of fabric 9 inches wide by the length of the yardage (24 inches).

Cut 6 inches from one end of the waistband strip for the inside change pockets. Divide into two pieces: 6 inches by 4½ inches.

2. Cut the remaining 24-by-36-inch segment in half, across the grain (two segments: 36 inches wide by 12 inches long). Mark the top of each piece to be sure you keep the grain running in the same direction on both pockets.

3. Prepare the tiny inner pockets. Fold and stitch a ¾-inch hem across the top of each segment. Fold and press a narrow hem around the other three sides. Center the small pocket on the wrong side of the fabric, 3 inches down from the top edge. Topstitch onto the large pocket before you close any seams.

4. Fold the large pocket in half, right sides together, matching the 12 inch sides. Sew the fabric into a tube as follows: Stitch down 2 inches from the top edge. Leave an opening of 5 to 6 inches and complete the seam to the bottom of the fabric (approximately 4 inches).

5. Press open the seam and center the stitching line on the fabric. Sew the bottom edge and turn pocket to right side.

6. Run gathering thread across the top edge, through both thicknesses of fabric.

7. Complete the second pocket to match.

PLEATED WAISTBAND

8. Starting 1½ inches from the cut edge of the fabric, pin and sew three ¼-inch tucks down the length of the band with the pleats to the outside.

Interface the entire waistband to give it a little extra body.

Mark the point, each side, where the band meets your side seam. Mark additional points: center back and center front (where the band overlaps).

9. Center the pockets over the side-seam marks, each side, along the cut edge of the waistband. Right sides of the fabric should be together. Gather the pocket tops slightly, leaving equal gaps across the center front and center back marks. Stitch pockets to the band.

10. Fold the band in half and sew the short ends together. Turn the waistband over the pockets and topstitch. Sew two 1-inch strips of matching Velcro within the overlap, parallel to the bottom edge, for an adjustable closure.

VARIATIONS: DESIGNS AND DETAILS

- Make a fabric rose or buy a nosegay of silk posies and wear them over the closure at the center of the waistband.

- Pin a special brooch over the closure of the waistband.

- Make a large, flat bow of matching or contrasting fabric and tack to the center of the waistband (Illus. 162).

- Tack a sequinned, embroidered or beaded butterfly to the shoulder of your plain black dress and make a simple overskirt to match one of the colors in the appliqué. This could be a real hit for the next dinner dance.

- Sew a China silk overskirt to match or contrast with last season's dress and listen to the compliments on your "new" dress at the next luncheon.

- Add a crepe pocket-peplum and matching bow tie to your favorite knit dress that is so comfortable for the office.

- Use seasonal trim to decorate an overskirt (Illus. 163). Red or green net sprinkled with holly leaves and berries will enhance the Christmas season for at-home entertaining or an evening out. Sequin eggs, little rabbits, pink, green and yellow grosgrain bows would be fun at Easter time. For patriotic celebrations you might consider red, white and blue for your net skirt. Decorate with flags, bright colored bows or glittery stars for the occasion. The trim can be secured with tiny safety pins for quick removal before laundering.

Illus. 162.

Any of these overskirts can be worn over a dress or pants. They can turn a jumpsuit into an at-home outfit or a simple skirt and matching top into a ball gown. Your only problem (if you can call it that) is that everyone will want to know where you find all these new clothes.

Try any of these suggestions or come up with some of your own. The design and finish of these overskirts can be as creative and inventive as you want them to be. When the party is over, they can be folded and tucked into a box on your closet shelf or kept in a drawer. No need for them to take up valuable closet space and get dusty from hanging.

Illus. 163.

Hats and Other Head Coverings

No matter how you define the word fashionable, the picture is incomplete without some sort of adornment for the head. Hats frame the face, call attention to your eyes, enhance a hairdo or complete a look (Illus. 164). Hats can be a major part of elegance.

Millinery has ridden the same fashion cycles as every other item of body covering. The difference is that where other bits of fashion come and go (some never to reappear) some form of head-covering seems to crop up every season.

Illus. 164.

Beret

The beret is claimed by the Scots, worn by the French, and loved by the Basques. It has been sported by men and women alike, and there almost seems to be an unwritten law that most children have a beret in their lives at some time. If overlooked during the early years, the beret often crowns the head of one in the "golden years."

Of all the head-coverings that have been designed, the beret has probably undergone the fewest changes of style. Its size has been affected, but what else can you do to change the wheel, once it has been invented?

A beret is a circle of fabric that is worn straight on the head or slanted to either side (Illus. 165). It is made from single or double fabric, lined, unlined or reversible. Fabric of choice can be sheer, translucent or opaque. Berets are made from solid colors, prints, patterns, stripes and plaids. They can have a drawstring, elastic or fitted band around the opening. Some even come with brims.

Unlined Beret

Make a simple, unlined beret of melton cloth or matted wool. Choose the color wisely because someone is sure to borrow it and forget to bring it back. The more personal the chosen color, the easier it is to identify your lost treasure.

Choose a substantial fabric that holds its shape and has enough body to look as if it belongs on your head, not in your pocket.

Illus. 165.

112

1. Measure your head size for a personally styled beret. Use one-half the actual measurement for the radius of the circle.

Spread the fabric on your cutting board. Pin the end of your tape measure to the board allowing enough room around the center point to stretch the tape to your chosen measurement (approximately 11½ inches). Draw a complete circle directly on the fabric. Use tailor's chalk or a sliver of soap for an erasable outline.

2. Cut around the marked line.

3. There are several ways to complete a beret:

1. Cut a length of grosgrain ribbon the measurement of your head plus 1 inch for overlap. Overlap the ribbon ends ½ inch each side and pin.

Sew a gathering thread around the outer edge of the fabric circle.

Pin the ribbon around the outside edge of the fabric and cinch the gathering thread to the measurement of your head. Sew. Turn the ribbon to the inside and topstitch close to the seam. The extra stitching provides a firm band for the hat and the raw edge of the fabric is encased (Illus. 166).

2. Cut the beret as described. Turn a narrow casing (½ inch) around the outside of the circle and stitch, leaving an opening through which you thread a length of ¼-inch, round elastic. Pull the elastic until it is comfortable around the head; not tight enough to cut off your circulation, nor so loose that the beret falls over the eyes. Secure the elastic and take a few stitches to close the entry slot (Illus. 167).

3. When you cut the fabric circle, cut a strip from the selvage, long enough to go around your head, plus ½-inch seam allowance. Tighten the gathering thread around the outside of the fabric and pin the strip to the hat, right sides together. Sew the band to the hat, turn to inside and stitch in the ditch to complete the hat and hide the raw edges of the circle (Illus. 168).

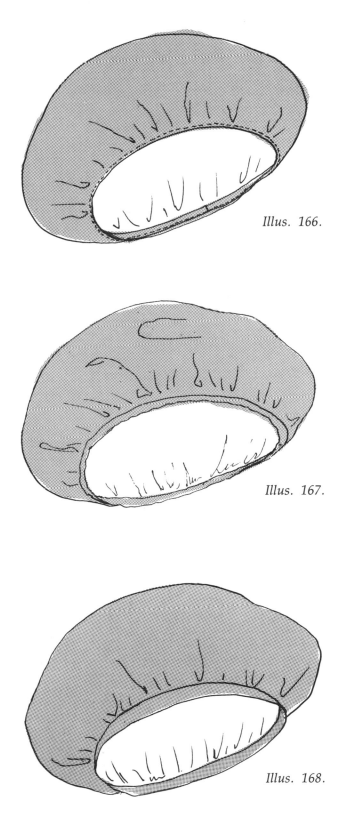

Illus. 166.

Illus. 167.

Illus. 168.

113

4. Sew a separate casing around the circle and run matching or contrasting ¼-inch ribbon through the opening. Cinch the ribbon to your head size and tie the ends with a bow or knot. For comfort, sew a 4-inch strip of ¼-inch elastic at the center of the ribbon.

Reversible Beret

Choose two contrasting fabrics for a reversible beret; one solid color, the other patterned or glittery with metallic thread for dressy occasions. This is a practical hat as it can be packed flat in a suitcase when you travel or hung on a hook when not being worn. Crush it at the bottom of your purse or in your desk drawer and it still comes up elegant.

1. Cut one 11½-inch circle from each piece of fabric.

2. Sew the two fabric circles with right sides together leaving a small opening through which to turn the fabric to the right side.

3. Topstitch around the beret, 1 inch in from the outer edge to form a casing for an elastic or a ribbon drawstring. Insert the ribbon, draw to head size and wear the hat at a jaunty angle.

Darted Beret

The darted beret is cut in a circle like the other styles, but it is not gathered to shape with elastic or drawstrings. This style is shaped to your head with a series of darts or pleats, then finished with a solid band.

Opt for a large, floppy, artist's style beret of velvet or velour.

1. Cut the fabric circle 24 to 28 inches in diameter.

2. Make ½-inch darts or pleats around the outer rim of the fabric: north, south, east and west. Add darts or pleats between the original four tucks until the beret fits to your head size (Illus. 169).

Illus. 169.

3. Cut two lengths of grosgrain ribbon for the sweatband and facing, ½ to ¾ inch larger than your actual head measurement.

Sew the band and facing together along one edge.

Stitch the sweatband to the outside of the beret, encasing the pleated or darted edge. Topstitch through all three layers of fabric.

Beret with Brim

Trace a pattern for a brim from any visor or cap. Cut two from matching fabric and interface both portions for a firm finish. Sew the brim around edge of the gathered (or darted) beret, between the body of the hat and the sweatband.

Attach two complete brims to a small beret for a deerstalker hat (Illus. 170). Overlap the outer points of the brims, if necessary.

Illus. 170.

Pie-Slice Large Beret

Cut a beret in a series of wedges or pie-shaped pieces of fabric or leather. The segments can match or contrast, come from scraps of the same fabric or an assortment of fabrics (Illus. 171).

Draft a pattern or template for the wedge to be sure that all segments are the same size and shape. Use a piece of pattern drafting paper or tagboard 14 inches by 6 inches.

Illus. 171.

1. Draw a 12-inch line down the middle of the paper. Mark the top. Measure down 9½ inches from that point and mark for the widest point of the wedge.

2. Along the bottom of the wedge measure 3¼ inches, evenly spaced across the center line. This is the return or inner ring of the beret.

3. At the widest point, measure 5¼ inches evenly across the center line.

4. Connect the outer points. Your pattern should look like this (Illus. 172).

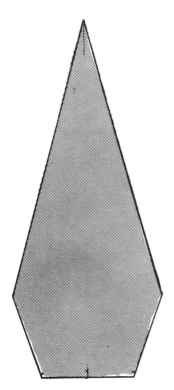

Illus. 172.

Label the pattern: *Cut Eight* (8). The pattern fits a 22-inch head size. There is a ¼-inch seam allowance included on all sides of the pattern piece.

If your head is **smaller** than 22 inches, sew the center-back segment(s) with a ½-inch (or more) seam allowance along the lower portion of the wedge to reduce the head size as much as needed.

If your head size is **larger** than 22 inches, add ¼ inch to each side of the back segments to reach the necessary measurements.

Ribbon Beret

Make a "go-everywhere" beret from embroidered, woven gilt or plain grosgrain ribbon (Illus. 173). This is a dressy pouf that looks as perfect with silks or tweeds as it does with knits and furs.

Illus. 173.

REQUIREMENTS

The design calls for 3⅓ yards of 3-inch wide ribbon.

Faille, brocade or a heavy jacquard fabric can be substituted for the ribbon if it is cut into 3-inch-wide strips to accommodate the pattern.

Narrower ribbon may be substituted. Sew two lengths of 1½-inch ribbon together to form 3-inch-wide strips for each row. Using narrow ribbon requires 6⅔ yards.

Cut the ribbon into the required lengths as follows:

ROW 1: 24 inches long.
ROW 2: 32 inches long.
ROW 3: 40 inches long.
ROW 4: 24 inches long (head size + 1 inch)

1. Sew the first strip of ribbon (24 inches) into a ring. French-seam the ends of the ribbon or use an overlock machine to prevent fraying.

Gather the ribbon tightly along one edge. There will be a small opening at the center and the fabric will lie in a flat circle (Illus. 174).

2. Sew the second strip of ribbon (32 inches) into a ring.

Pin it around the outside of the first strip, taking small tucks every 3 to 4 inches to fit the two strips together.

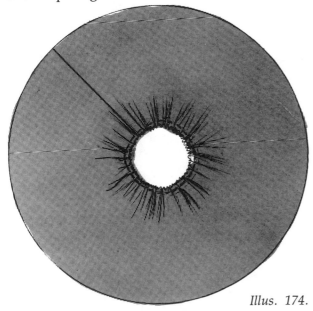

Illus. 174.

Sew the two strips together with a zigzag or overlapping stitch, just barely butting the two edges of the ribbon together.

3. Sew the third strip (40 inches) into a ring.

First pin, then sew it to the outside of the second ring as above. All three rows should lie fairly flat.

4. Take a series of ½-inch tucks, approximately 3 inches apart, around the outside of the last ring of ribbon. This bends the outside edge in towards the center, forming the return of the beret. Add darts as needed to fit your head size.

5. The fourth strip (24 inches) is the sweatband. Pin the ends together and wrap it around your head to be sure it fits comfortably. Allow a little slack as sewing the band to the hat will draw up the fabric. Sew the ends together and pin the band around the bottom edge of the beret, right sides together. Try the hat on to scan the arrangement of the pleats. Make any necessary adjustments before you sew the band to the hat.

There are two ways to finish the band: (a) Fold the entire band to the inside and top-stitch all the way around, as close to the edge as possible. No part of the band is visible when worn. (b) Fold the band towards the inside and stitch, just barely enclosing the edge of the last row of ribbon. This forms a visible band that shows below the pouf of the beret.

VARIATION: BERET FROM NARROW RIBBON

A similar hat can be made with 2-inch ribbon. This pattern makes up into a slightly larger beret than the first one.

REQUIREMENTS

With a single sweatband: 5⅓ yards of 2-inch ribbon.

With a double sweatband: 6 yards of 2-inch ribbon.

MEASUREMENTS

Row 1: 22 inches

Row 2: 28 inches

Row 3: 34 inches

Row 4: 40 inches

Row 5: 45 inches

Band: 23 inches

1. Cut the ribbon to the required lengths and sew into rings as in previous version.

2. Gather one long edge of the first row as tightly as possible.

3. Pin the second ring of ribbon under the edge of the first. Take tucks in the top edge of the second strip to make the two pieces fit together. Overlap the edges as little as possible (approximately ⅛ inch). Sew on conventional machine using a straight stitch.

Complete all rows as above.

4. If you planned on a single sweatband, sew it to the outside of the beret, right sides together. Turn in and topstitch.

If you planned on a self-faced band for the hat, sew the two lengths of ribbon together (24-inches), along one edge, wrong sides together. Pin around the tucked edge of the beret, encasing the pleated rim. Make any adjustments necessary to make the top portion of the beret and the band fit together neatly. Topstitch through all thicknesses.

5. An ornamental cockade is a nice trim for the hatband (Illus. 175). Cut a square of matching ribbon and sew a circular gathering stitch around the edge into a circle.

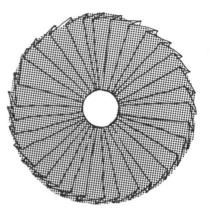

Illus. 175.

Fill with cotton batting or fabric scraps to hold the shape of the ball. Pull up the gathering thread.

Cut 10 to 12 inches of ribbon, pleat and fold it to fit around the outside of the center ball and tack in place.

Sew a safety pin to the center back (Illus. 176).

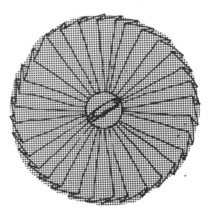

Illus. 176.

EXTRA ADDED ATTRACTIONS

- Your beret may be further shaped by adding a clip or brooch at one side.

- Pin a cockade of matching ribbon (with streamers added) to one side of the band (Illus. 177). Let the ribbon ends flow over your shoulder or secure them to your lapel with a matching cockade.

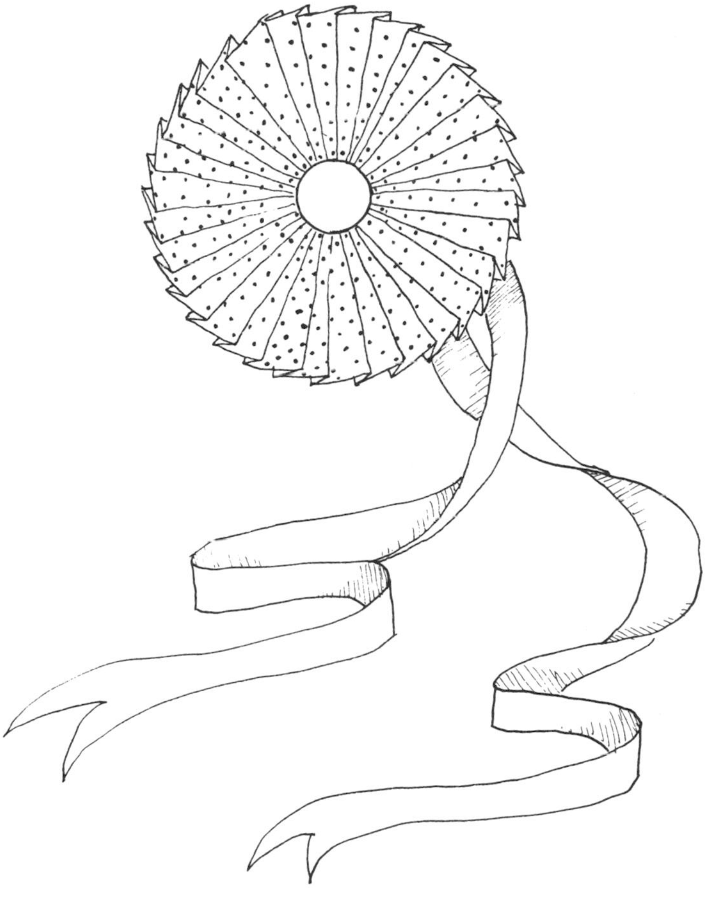

Cocktail Hats

Cocktail hats are designed to serve absolutely no practical use. They grace the head purely for decorative purposes, like a bow on a gift box (Illus. 178). They are too small to hide a bad hairdo and too large to be considered something resting there by accident. They're a definite asset at stand-up parties—cocktail hats are always conversation openers.

Horsehair braid makes up into a flirty head topping, much like frosting on a wedding cake. A medium-size comb, 1/3 yard of heavy mesh for a face veil, and approximately 2 yards of horsehair braid (purchased at either your favorite fabric shop or local craft store) and you're on your way to a delicate cocktail hat to top an evening costume.

Illus. 177.

Illus. 178.

DIRECTIONS

1. Fold a length of 3-inch-wide horsehair braid into three or more large loops (Illus. 179). Fold approximately 9 inches of braid into each loop. Gather across the center of each loop slightly to hold the puffy shape.

Cut the flat ends of the braid on the bias to incorporate them into the design of the bow.

2. Gather or pleat the veil along one long side.

Choose a comb that will stay in your hair; There are many types available and not all combs work for every type of hair.

Take three or four whipstitches through the veil, around the top of the comb, and between the teeth, using a needle and double thread to hold the mesh in place (Illus. 180).

3. Tack the bow on top of the veil. Sew through the fabric and stitch as above.

4. Wear this little hat well to the front with the veil just grazing the eyebrows (Illus. 181).

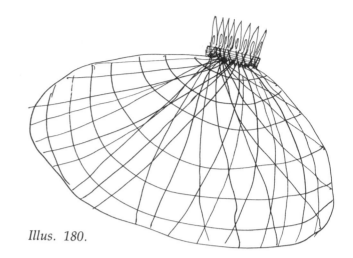

Illus. 180.

Illus. 181.

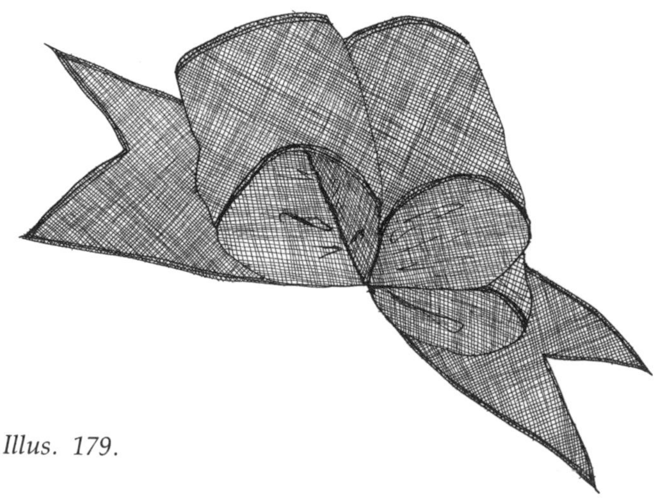

Illus. 179.

120

Cabbage Rose Hat

The fabric flowers you made (directions on page 124) are perfect for a grand-entrance cocktail hat. Try them in tulle or voile for a stunning effect. Choose your colors carefully as this little hat sits right above your eyebrows and is a real attention-getter. Let it compliment your complexion as well as your eyes.

DIRECTIONS

1. Make two large cabbage roses from voile (details page 124).

2. Sew two or three rhinestones to the flowers at random spots for a little extra glitter.

3. Cut five fat, squatty leaf shapes and finish the outer edges.
   Arrange them around and between the two roses.

4. Tack the leaves underneath the finished flowers and sew to a comb.

Wear the finished hat well forward on the head with the leaves draped over the forehead (Illus. 182). This is a very special-occasion hat.
   Substitute five small roses for the two large ones. These can also be made from voile or tulle, or you might try your hand at ribbon roses. Follow the same directions for wrapping the fabric to shape but hold the base securely in one hand as you wrap; you don't have to tack the ribbon between layers. Sew or glue the ends in place.
   Make seven leaves to sprinkle between the roses.
   Sew to a comb for use on the top of the head; use a piece of round elastic to wear these roses around a pony tail.

Illus. 182.

Variation on the Visor

The pattern you drafted for the visor (Beret with Brim, page 115) can be used for another style of hat, a sort of tiara. Turn the visor upside down, let the rounded portion point up, and you have an open crowned hat that lends itself to an assortment of wonderful fabrics (Illus. 183). Make it from brocade or metallic cloth for evening, prints or embroidered fabric for daytime wear. It has a totally adjustable head size: it closes with a strip of Velcro tape. Adapt this bit of millinery to match or blend with any outfit and wear a truly unusual bit of millinery.

Illus. 183.

DIRECTIONS

Use the visor pattern you drafted for the beret. Extend the outer points of the curve to meet the measurement of your head plus 1½ inches for overlap.

1.   Cut two from your visor pattern. This can be a reversible style if the segments are cut from contrasting fabric.

2.   Interface both the outer portion and the facing for a little extra firmness. Do any appliqué or jewelling before putting the outer fabric and facings together.

3.   Sew around the roundly curved portion of the visor with right sides together. Leave an opening on the opposite side to turn the fabric.
   Turn the fabric to the right side and topstitch over the slit.

4.   Sew Velcro tape to the overlapping ends.

Ribbons and Bows

Adorning the hair with ribbons is not a new concept; it has been done through the ages. What makes it new today is how these things are used in the hair. Rosettes made from lace edging, with or without the addition of ¼-inch satin ribbon streamers, feathers of all kinds sewn to combs or clips, thongs strung with beads, ribbon bows to suggest the season, all worn in multiples, all adding to a festive atmosphere. Plain rubber bands, bobby pins or clippies will hold back your hair, but why not wear something pretty?

*   One yard of ½-inch plaid or print ribbon will make six pretty bows. Cut the length of ribbon into six equal pieces. Form the bows and tie each one to a double-ended clippy for hair control where you want it. Clip all the bows around a chignon or pony tail (Illus. 184).
   Substitute bobby pins and bows for a tighter hold on fine hair. Pin them across the crown of your head or circle some curls at the nape of your neck.

*   Attach small flowers to clips and wear them in groups of three or more (Illus. 185). Add streamers of ribbon or lace.

*   Fold ¾ yard of 3-inch velvet or brocade ribbon into a large bow. Wrap the center with a few inches of matching ¼-inch ribbon and sew the center band to an oversize bobby pin. Wear straight on the top of the head (Illus. 186).

Be inventive with hair accessories. When you put forth the effort to create a pretty hairdo, add something to enhance it, and put extra sparkle in your eyes. You wouldn't serve a birthday cake without frosting and candles.

Illus. 184.

Illus. 185.

Illus. 186.

FABRIC FLOWERS AND LEAVES

Flowers have been celebrated in poetry and song throughout time. They have been the focus of artists, sculptors and craftsmen, knitters, weavers and quilters. Fashion designers and fabric makers have joined to create entire collections in praise of simple garden flowers.

The cabbage rose is considered a romantic flower but it does have a rather short growing season. Make a cabbage rose of fabric and it will last forever. It has an imposing appearance and adds a touch of color to your clothing. Once you learn how easy they are to complete, you'll find yourself using this technique to create your own garden for everything from personal accessories to home decorating.

Cabbage Rose

SUGGESTED FABRIC

Nylon voile, silk, net or tulle. Solid colors, stripes or prints.

DIRECTIONS

The basic principle involved in creating a cabbage rose is pleating and wrapping the fabric to produce a controlled pouf.

1.   Cut a strip of nylon voile approximately 12 inches long by the width of the fabric (64 inches).

2.   Fold the strip into three equal portions and cut along the fold lines. Each strip should measure approximately 12 inches wide by 21 inches long (+ or − 1 inch).

3.   Make a bias fold at one corner of the first strip. Match the side and bottom edges (Illus. 187).

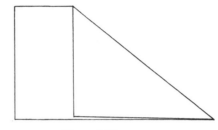

Illus. 187.

Fold the corner over approximately ½ inch, starting from the point and wrap three or four times to create a firm base for the center of the rose (Illus. 188).

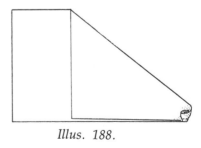

Illus. 188.

Tack the rolled corner with a few large stitches, ¼ inch from the raw edge to prevent the center from unrolling.

124

4. Make one or two pleats next to the base, along the raw edge, approximately 1 inch deep. Tack these folds to the base.

Continue to pleat and tack the fabric (to prevent it from unrolling) until you come to the corner of the first fold (Illus. 189).

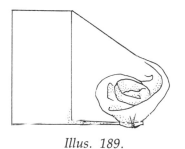

Illus. 189.

5. Secure the point to the wrapped portion and bring the raw side of the fabric down to match the other edge. Gather, pleat and tack the remaining fabric as above, until you reach the opposite end, and all pleats and folds have been secured (Illus. 190).

Illus. 190.

Be sure to finish the rose attractively. The outer layer of the flower is obviously the most visible and should be finished generously.

Take a critical look at your flower before you tack down the final row of pleating. Decide whether you are satisfied with the shape. It's easier to undo the last few pleats and puff the outer layer of fabric to your satisfaction before taking the finishing stitches. If you think the rose looks a little flat, repleat as much as necessary to achieve the look you want. The finished rose should have pleasing roundness and be very luxuriant (see Illus. 191).

Illus. 191.

Make one to three leaves to complete the rose. (See Leaf Collar, page 131 for directions.)

Small Roses

Make smaller sized roses to use in groups of three or more for neckline, waistline or lapel.

1. Cut a strip from the fabric, 3 inches wide by the entire width.

2. Sew the strip into a tube, using a serger or overlock machine. (Where no serger is available, substitute a serging stitch or zigzag stitch on a conventional sewing machine.)

3. Fold the fabric tube into three equal parts and separate the segments. Each small tube will measure approximately 1½ inches by 15 inches (+ or −).

125

4. Bias-fold one end and wrap to form a center core. Continue to wrap and tack the entire strip (as explained above), until the entire length of the tube is secured.

Keep the tube as even as possible, with the seam line at the bottom of the flower.

5. Make three to five leaves to finish the rose. (See Leaves, Fabric Flowers, page 132.)

Attach the leaves to the rose as you complete the last winding. Pleat the cut end of the leaf and place that portion against the flower. The pointed end of the leaf hangs down (Illus. 192). Tack each leaf in place as you sew the final winding of the rose.

6. A small circle of fabric is sewn over the wrapped and stitched base of the flower. Sew a small safety pin to the base covering.

SUGGESTIONS FOR USE

Larger size roses are made from fabric yardage; smaller roses can be made either from sheer fabric, material that matches a specific garment or ribbon.

Flowers made from ribbon are limited in size to the width of the ribbon chosen. The smaller sizes can be used in much the same way as the larger ones; they're just not as showy. Use more of the little ribbon flowers to get the extravagant effect the large sizes achieve with fabric yardage.

- Pin a rose to the lapel of your jacket. It softens the look of very tailored clothing (Illus. 193).

Illus. 192.

Illus. 193.

- Close the collar of your shirt with one large or three small roses (Illus. 194). They can match or contrast with the shirt.

- Roses at the waistline are a feminine finish for dress or skirt (Illus. 195).

- See Hats and Other Head Covering (page 111) for additional suggestions.

Illus. 194.

Illus. 195.

Lazy Daisies

The daisy is a quieter, more subtle flower than the rose. Though it serves a similar purpose: adorning your basics, it is a more tailored decoration.

Daisy petals are made in a manner similar to that used in making leaves, with one minor change: The petals are made in a string (like a child's string of paper dolls) instead of being cut into strips and completed separately (Illus. 196). Stitch them on the serger or with a conventional sewing machine.

Illus. 197.

3. Using contrasting or matching thread, feed the strip through the overlock machine, finishing off the rounded edges only (Illus. 198). If there is no serger available, sew on a conventional sewing machine.

Turn all petals to the right side, concealing the stitching.

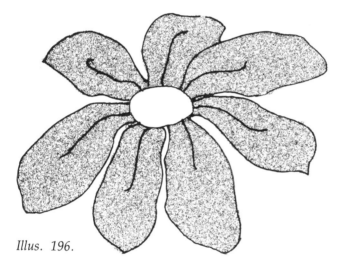

Illus. 196.

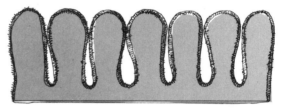

Illus. 198.

DIRECTIONS: METHOD #1

1. Cut a strip of fabric 7 inches long by the width of the yardage. Fold the fabric in half (approximately 7 by 18 inches) to sew the flower double.

2. Fan-pleat the entire width of the fabric to approximately 3 by 7 inches (Illus. 197). Round off one end with a scissor, leaving the opposite end connected.

4. Cut a 3-inch circle of fabric for the center of the flower. Sew a gathering thread approximately ½ inch from the edge. Stuff with cotton balls or tiny scraps from the fabric, cinch the gathering thread and tie off.

5. Place the string of petals against the padded base, matching the bottom edges. Fold each petal (in turn) down the center and wrap the pleats against the base (Illus. 199).

Tack one folded petal at a time, just letting each one meet the last. Widen or narrow the pleats where necessary to balance the petals. Each petal will stand away from the next.

Illus. 199.

DIRECTIONS: METHOD #2

When the scrap fabric is too small to cut the petals in a continuous strip, make six or seven separate petals.

1.   Cut separate petals from double-fabric approximately 3 by 5 inches. If you are sewing them with a serger, shape each petal as you sew.

Completing the flower on a conventional sewing machine, cut each petal to a leaf-shape: rounded at the top, sides tapering towards the bottom edge, and straight across the bottom (Illus. 200).

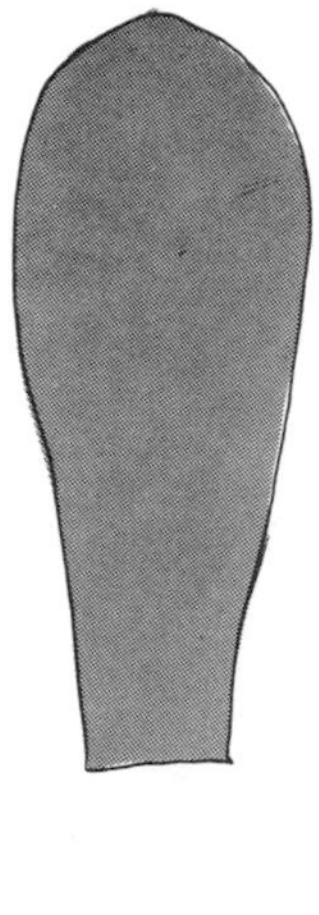

Illus. 200.

2.   Cut a circular base, approximately 2 to 3 inches in diameter. Sew a running stitch around the edge of the fabric, stuff with cotton, and cinch the gathering thread. Take a few extra stitches across the opening to completely secure the ball.

3.   Hand-stitch the petals to the ball, one at a time. Take a vertical tuck at the bottom of each petal as you pin it to the ball. Tack each one around the center, keeping the base flat at the bottom. Overlap the petals slightly as you sew, then stitch around the completed flower base to tighten all petals. Keep the bottom edges of all petals even (Illus. 201). It takes about six or seven petals to complete the daisy.

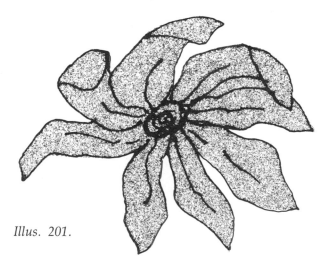

Illus. 201.

Sew larger sized daisies for the fun of it; cutting and construction methods are the same as described, no matter how large the petals. Petals should measure approximately 8 to 10 inches in length.

SUGGESTIONS FOR USE

Fabric daisies are very adaptable: use them to trim a hat, complete a belt, or decorate an evening gown (Illus. 202). Sew them to the side of a tote bag or the shoulder of a T-shirt.

Use one or more to secure a scarf. Spark the neckline of a blouse by using a daisy instead of a tie at the collar.

Daisies work well from almost any fabric; They certainly use up scraps. For more versatility with pin-on daisies, make the petals from a variety of fabrics left over from favorite garments. Change fabric between the center and petals or alternate fabric for the petals.

Illus. 202.

Leaf Collar

The leaf collar is a sophisticated accessory that adds froth and glamour to a simple dress, suit or blouse. It embellishes an afternoon ensemble, cocktail outfit or evening wear (Illus. 203).

The finished collar has a highly detailed appearance when worn but is actually very simple to make.

SUGGESTED FABRIC

Nylon voile or other firmly woven, sheer, fabric.

REQUIREMENTS

½ yard nylon voile
Matching or contrasting thread
1½″ Velcro tape

DIRECTIONS

Neckband. Prepare the neckband first. The finished leaves are arranged on the band.

Illus. 203.

1. Cut a single neckband 5 by 17 inches (or long enough to go completely around the neck and overlap approximately 1 inch, without binding.

2. Fold band in half down the length. Pin in a ½-inch seam allowance at both ends.

Fold and press a ½-inch seam along the raw edges.

Leaves. The collar uses a *minimum* of 18 leaf-shaped segments. More can be added as desired.

1. Cut leaf shapes freehand to give a fluffier appearance to the finished collar. Use a template for more regular or even leaves.

2. All leaves are approximately the same width, between 2½ and 3 inches wide. Vary the finished lengths of the leaves for this outstanding accessory:

5 long leaves approximately 10 to 12 inches in length.
7 medium leaves approximately 7 to 8 inches long.
9 small leaves approximately 5 to 6 inches long.

3. Fanfold a 10-inch strip of fabric into five or more segments approximately 3 inches wide. Rough-cut the large leaf shape and separate all segments (Illus. 204).

Illus. 204.

4. Sew around each leaf singly, using a serger or overlock machine to outline each petal with stitching.

Fold the hemmed petal in half and stitch down the length ½ to ¾ of the way to the point (Illus. 205). Trim all loose threads. Where a serger is not available substitute the serging stitch on a conventional sewing machine to overcast the raw edges of the fabric as you sew.

Illus. 205.

Continue with the medium and small-size leaves until all are completed. Keep them separated into size groups; it makes it easier to plan the layout of the petals.

FINISHING DETAILS

1. Lay the collarband on a table and place the three separate piles of leaves in a nearby, convenient location.

2. Start by placing the longest leaf at the center of the neckband (Illus. 206). Pin it between the two layers of the folded collarband.

3. Space the remaining 10-to-12-inch leaves across the width of the band.

4. Intersperse the medium-size leaves between the large leaves.

5. Arrange the small leaves last. Overlap the larger sizes and fill in the spaces.

6. Pin each of the segments in place individually and try the collar around your neck. The petals fall over the top of the collarband with the shortest petals on top, the longest dan-

gling underneath. Rearrange the petals (if necessary) until all segments fall nicely over the shoulders, front and back.

7. When you are satisfied with the arrangement, topstitch the band (with the leaves between the fold of the fabric). Use a conventional sewing machine.
Stitch the ends of the collarband.

8. Add snaps, hooks and eyes or Velcro tape at the back within the overlap.

Wear this sophisticated collar over a high or low neckline. It is as handsome over the bare skin as it is over fabric, topping a turtleneck.

Illus. 206.

DECORATIONS THAT GLITTER

Glitter and glitz never really go out of style. Glamour knows no age, size or limits. A season's fashion trend just varies the amount of each that is acceptable.

There is no rule-of-thumb for the amount of glittery additives that can be strewn over a costume. No one can advise you on how much gilding can be added to the lily before it becomes too much; this is a matter of personal taste. The only known guideline is, *If you want to shine, Shine!!!*

A simple dress can glow with a tie-on bib encrusted with silver and/or gold nailheads, sequins or rhinestones (Illus. 207). A beaded or sequinned vest will change that same sheath into a knockout ensemble. Substitute a gleaming overskirt or peplum that has been strewn with sequins, beads and motifs and you temporarily glamorize that sheath into a one-of-a-kind costume that is a real standout. Brilliant accessories are the answer when the dressing problem involves shimmer and

Illus. 207.

134

shine. There is no limit to what sparkle will do for your wardrobe—and your ego.

Sequins provide the maximum amount of glitter for the amount of effort involved in decorating a garment. They can be purchased in several forms: Loose sequins that are attached individually, strings of sequins that are spiraled or draped across a bodice or skirt, and finished motifs that are completed patterns, suitable for individual use or in groups.

SEQUINS: GENERAL INFORMATION

Sew sequins by hand; machine-sewing will break more sequins than you attach. Use a matching or neutral color thread that will not show up too obviously in the finished pattern. Tack the individual sequins or strings loosely to prevent puckering the fabric.

Single sequins can be sewn individually by one of two methods.

WITH A BEAD

Secure sequins to the fabric by sewing a bead at the center of each one to hold it flat to the garment. Beads come in tubes or small packages and are available in all colors including gold and silver. Choose a size just large enough to cover the hole at the center of the sequin without slipping through.

You can use multicolored beads to create patterns within a sequinned motif. Study the bead color carefully to complement the effect you're trying to achieve. Matching beads are almost invisible, contrasting beads can shade or tone the pattern for a completely different effect.

1.   Knot the sewing thread and bring the needle up from the wrong side of the fabric, through the center hole of the sequin.

2.   String a tiny bead and reinsert the needle through the same hole in the sequin. Pull the needle through to the wrong side of the fabric firmly enough to hold the sequin and bead to the fabric without puckering the fabric.

3.   Bring the needle back to the right side of the fabric, allowing enough space from the first for the second sequin to lie flat (Illus. 208). String the sequin and bead, and again, return to the underside of the fabric through the center of the sequin.

Illus. 208.

Tie a single knot after every three or four sequins to prevent the entire string from pulling out if the thread should break.

Once you get started you'll have a better feel for the thread tension and the spacing of the sequins. Continue in this fashion until the pattern is completed.

WITHOUT A BEAD

Individual sequins are attached by sewing the first one flat to the garment and overlapping all succeeding sequins. This looks similar to prestrung sequins but is more secure; everything won't fall off if a knot comes undone.

Attach sequins with one technique or another, or intersperse both styles of sewing to enhance the pattern. The overlap method of application prevents the thread from showing within the design.

1. Bring the threaded needle from the back of the fabric to the front.

2. Pick up a sequin with the point of the needle. Slide the sequin down the thread to the fabric.

3. Take a tiny stitch over the outer edge of the first sequin. Thread a second sequin and again, tack just barely over the outer edge. The sequins will overlap, completely hiding the sewing thread (Illus. 209). Sew loosely to prevent the motif from puckering.

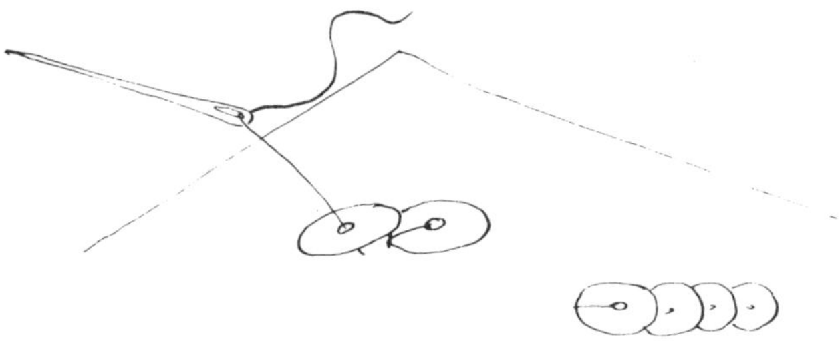

Illus. 210.

Plan the pattern you want the sequins to follow. Twist and turn the string of sequins to fill in the shape of the design you have chosen. Baste the string to the fabric. Hide the thread under the overlapping edges as you sew.

Illus. 209.

SEQUIN STRINGS

Sequins are also available in chain-stitched, overlapped strings. They are available in many colors and require less sewing than individual sequins. Sequin strings can be purchased by the yard at fabric and craft shops (Illus. 210).

SEQUINNED AND JEWELLED MOTIFS

Fabric shops often carry presequinned appliqués that can be tacked to finished garments either singly or in scattered groups. They are a little pricey but for a fast pick-me-up, there's nothing better. Large designs, such as floral bouquets, birds or animal, patriotic motifs (stars, stripes, flags, eagles, bolts of lightning, etc.) and almost anything else you can think up can be sewn to a finished dress in a matter of minutes. Add them to a sweater, dress, pants, jacket or overskirt and you have instant glamour.

Hand-sew sequinned motifs to keep all sequins and jewels intact. Whipstitch around each pattern, keeping the stitches hidden under the edge of the appliqué.

RHINESTONES AND LARGE JEWELS

Large stones can be sewn directly to the fabric. Many come predrilled with holes large enough to accept a needle (Illus. 211). Small stones such as rhinestones and little colored jewels come with findings that poke through the fabric and bend over the edges of the faceted stones (Illus. 212). There are little hand tools available at craft stores that save your fingertips and make the task of setting stones much simpler.

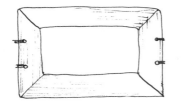

Illus. 211.

Illus. 212.

STARDUST

There is a glitter dust that you can buy at almost any craft shop and even some fabric shops. It looks like ground sequins and only needs some fabric glue to adhere to the garment. It is a fast and fun way to decorate clothing from evening gowns to sweatsuits and aerobic wear.

First plan your design. You must know where you want to use this treatment as it is difficult to remove once the glue dries.

Use a glue pen or a tube of fabric glue to trace around the pattern. Sprinkle the glitter from the bag over the wet outline. Don't get carried away and dump the whole bag in one little spot. You can always add more glitter to any area that looks too sparse, so don't overdo it at the start.

Allow the sprinkled outline to dry. Shake off the excess glitter and take a close look at the pattern. Fill in any areas that need more sparkle or add more details to the general design. When you are satisfied that your pattern is complete, gather up all the loose stardust and rebag it for future use. Loose glitter is always reusable.

This treatment is successful for knits or woven fabrics. It is a wonderful way to make health-club sweats into designer warm-ups with minimal investment. Try this technique on jeans and denim jackets. Give a denim skirt a new look.

There is another form of glitter: paint sticks. These come in assorted colors, plain or metallic. They are somewhat like ball-point pens; just remove the cap and draw. You can create a metallic painting on the garment of your choice and wear it immediately as these are quick-dry colors.

If your local fabric shop can't supply the items mentioned in this chapter, look in the yellow pages of your telephone directly for a craft store or dance costume supply shop. These are some of the best places in which to find inspiration. They have everything you need to reach new heights of decorative finishing for your accessory wardrobe.

QUILTED JEWELRY

You can buy all sorts of interesting costume jewelry pieces, but have you given any thought to the wonderful things you can create at your sewing machine? You don't need exotic wood and metal to create a jewelry collection that will rival the efforts of any of the current designers. You can make wonderful accent pieces from everyday fabric, and it's the easiest way to bring an assortment of your best colors close to your face.

A recent fashion emphasis on the safari look has animals, flora and fauna roaming through the most coveted boutiques in the world. Necklaces, bracelets and earrings sport everything from wild animals to palm trees and exotic foliage (Illus. 213). Create your own game preserve for a fraction of what it would cost to buy these items. Design a wearable zoo, or sew an ever-fresh lei of tropical flowers. Wear a string of mountains or a lovely seascape,

Illus. 213.

happy toy trains, or whatever your whim. Make one or make a dozen; these pieces are as much fun to wear as they are to dream up.

INSPIRATION AND SOURCE MATERIAL

Try drawing your own designs for quilted jewelry. It's lots of fun, creating your own birds, fish, animals or other critters. If they seem a little strange, all the better. They don't actually have to swim or fly.

If all else fails, the place to find very basic designs that will easily translate into sewable pieces is in children's coloring books. The drawings are simple, the lines are strong. They are easy to machine embroider and accent with glittery decorations or embroidery.

Magazines and/or newspapers are also excellent sources for designs. Use tissue or tracing paper and a soft pencil to copy the patterns.

GENERAL DIRECTIONS

1. Trace the simple outlines from your designs to fabric. Assorted objects: animal, vegetable or mineral, are adaptable to working designs. Choose simple, extended forms that can be connected on a string or in a row (Illus. 214). Leaping animals, flowers with stems, or reclining figures work best as they are stretched out, already reaching and easy to connect.

Vertical figures can be hung from metal or fabric rings (Illus. 215). Don't get too complicated or overly detailed with your basic designs as it won't translate well at the sewing machine.

2. Cut your beasties from fabric that lends itself to decorations: muslin, cotton, or metallic fabric, preferably plain to start with. Once you are comfortable with the technique of machine embroidery, choose some small prints to embellish.

Illus. 214.

139

Illus. 215.

3. Lightly stuff each motif. Sew around the design, quilting the pattern from the center out. Use your sewing machine needle as though you were drawing the details with pen or pencil.

Detail the front of each figure; the back can either be the plain fabric or a reverse design of the top.

4. Baste around the outside edge of each segment with a long, loose machine stitch. Follow around the edges a second time with a satin stitch in matching or contrasting color.

5. A horizontal design can be worked as a single unit. Cut the entire design and work out from the center in both directions until the pattern is completed. Attach ribbon, colored cord or soutache braid to each end of the quilted piece (Illus. 216). Tie in a bow or knot to wear.

Vertical segments that cannot be connected are completed and attached to the cord individually. Where possible, string motifs together and attach each piece or group to the cord with a thread or ribbon loop (Illus. 217).

140

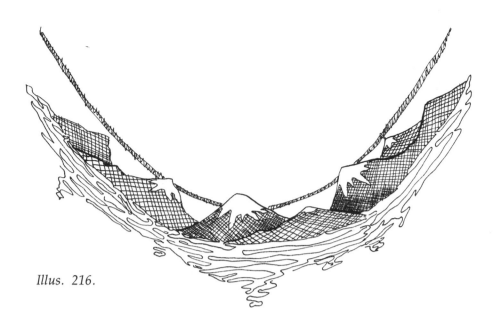

Illus. 216.

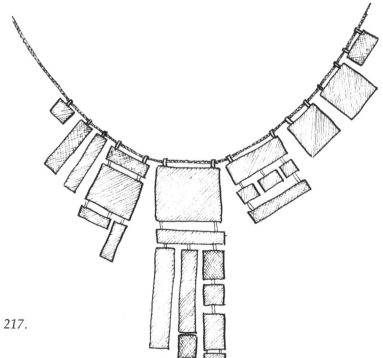

Illus. 217.

141

Illus. 218.

Cut the cord long enough to comfortably circle the neck, adding enough length to wear the necklace either high (like a choker) or low (about opera length).

- Find an assortment of exotic alphabets in embroidery books at your local fabric or craft shops. Trace the letters to keep the pages intact for future use. Spell out your name or short phrases in individual letters (Illus. 218). Embroider, sequin or jewel each letter.

  Cut each letter from a different print or patterned fabric, metallic, brocade or jacquard.

- There are many drawings and photographs of birds and fish in the encyclopedia or dictionary; another area that deserves a little research. Add real feathers to the birds, sequins are a good substitute for fish scales. Extra attention to your designs result in truly unusual pieces.

- No one ever outgrows the joys of the circus. Drape a tumbling team or a group of high-wire experts around your neck (Illus. 219).

  Opt for the ringmaster with his top hat and red coat, directing activities.

  Enjoy a string of small circus wagons, three for each side. Hang a replica of the main tent at the center (Illus. 220).

142

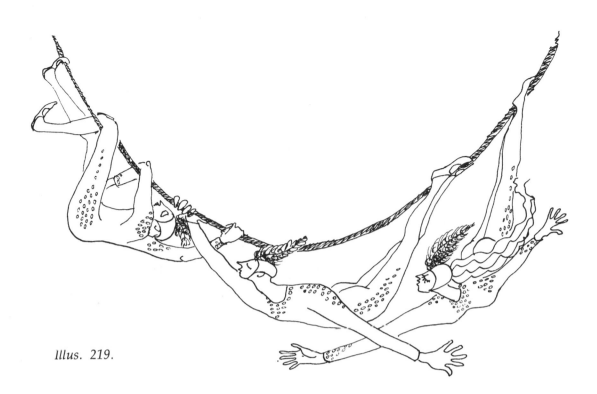

Illus. 219.

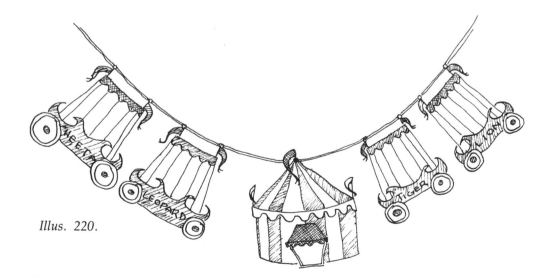

Illus. 220.

143

- You adore your house pet(s), are an avid bird watcher or eager gardener—one who wants the world to know about that hobby—or maybe you just like to wear fun jewelry. Cut around patterns from printed fabric that depict your major interest(s).

  Create a floral display that will never fade or die, a garden that never needs weeding, a menagerie that never has to be fed or groomed, or a fleet of boats that never have to be moored.

- Create necklaces with one or more lines of nursery rhyme characters or some of your favorites from old fairy tales. Start with a crescent moon and a sophisticated cow. (She can sit atop the crescent with crossed knees.) Hang a series of odd shaped stars underneath. A few rhinestones and sequins for a little glitter and you've started a collection of nursery rhyme jewelry for adults.

You might prefer an ice blue satin cloud topped by a full circle: a silver or white moon—and even add a cat and a fiddle.

- How are you fixed for rainbows? A rainbow is a delightful adornment, with or without clouds or pots of gold.

- Cut a kindergarten-style chain of paper dolls that curve gently around the neck (Illus. 221). Enjoy these wonderful children without any of the responsibility ordinarily connected with little kids. These children need absolutely no care beyond an occasional dunking in soap suds.

- Make some daisies that hang from a green silk cord. A few leaves to embellish the stalk would be attractive.

- Hang a small daisy blossom and a random assortment of loose petals for a graphic of: "He loves me, he loves me not." This conversation piece can be worn at the waist,

Illus. 221.

neckline, or wrist. To make it work well as a belt, add enough separate petals to hang completely around the waistline. Suspend each petal from its own, individual ring. They can all be bunched together when worn about the neck.

- Design a crest to pin on a jacket or sweater. It can be a solid shield or composed of small, decorated pieces (Illus. 222).

Illus. 222.

- Everyone loves balloons. Make yours of brightly colored cotton or metallic cloth. Tie them with gold or silver soutache braid or cord to keep them from flying away.

  Sequin a series of circles for a cluster of balloons. (See Decorations that Glitter, page 134) Bunch them on one side of the neck cord. Attach gold braid to each circle and drape the ends across the center of the necklace. Tie the ends to a large ring (Illus. 223).

  Attach some sequinned balloons to a pin-back for a shimmery brooch.

  Glue earring backs to a pair of sequin circles and wear them at your ears . . . all fun stuff.

Any of the above can adorn your neckline, wrist or waist if you make the tie-cord long enough. Make sure you cut the supporting cord long enough to go around your waist with enough length to tie. When worn around the neck, the ends hang down at the back.

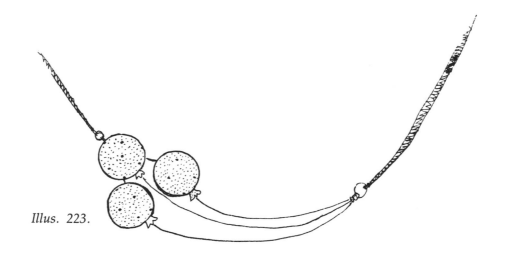

Illus. 223.

These are fun to wear and inspire lots of conversation. The best part: When they get dirty, pop them in the washer and dryer.

Take this jewelry on your next trip and you won't have to give a thought to putting your treasures in the safe when they're not being worn, and they won't add weight to your luggage.

- Use these same ideas to appliqué designs on a scarf, vest, skirt or jacket.

- Appliqué and/or machine-embroider these designs around the hemline of a blanket-coat or your favorite tweed skirt. All are fun additions to your wardrobe.

Epilogue: Fashion and Fancy

A child travels freely through the private world of imaging, and imagination. A curtain draped over the head, a bouquet of dandelions picked in a nearby empty lot and you were a bride, gliding down a carpeted aisle, all eyes focused on you.

Several strands of beads around your neck, a pair of hoops at your ears—and you were a grown-up, dancing beside a gypsy fire (Illus. 224).

What you instinctively did as a child was express a mood, create an aura, conjure up a secret image. You lived within a private vision, and you dreamed wonderful dreams of how you wanted to look. Then you tried to bring these dreams to life. (Illus. 224).

Childhood is a simple time when style flowers in the imagination and the ultimate in chic descends gracefully from a movie or television screen. It is a time when any cast-off that comes to hand becomes splendid, modish, and elegant. It is a time of fantasy, a time without doubts or inhibitions. Where does it go?

Think back to your childhood: the attitude of independence, the feeling of confidence, the joy of creating your own style.

Dealing with fashion isn't really any different today than it was in the time before you were an adult; the difference is the state of mind. Adults distrust natural instincts, shun invention and are embarrassed by imagination. It's easier to ignore creativity and deny the challenge of taking fashion risks. There is a reluctance to step away from the comfort of the pack and assert individuality. The anonymity of the school uniform is so easy, so neutral, *and* so boring.

Illus. 224.

Take another look at today's style. Give it some space in your life and allow it to tempt you. Recreate those earlier times not only in your clothing, but in the accessories that make your choices work.

Today's fashion is free. It is movement: the ebb and flow of beautiful fabric, the staccato of color, texture and pattern. It is simple; a new canvas waiting for your personal statement.

Today's fashion is eclectic—an assortment of separates that come together in a personal way. It is quality classics still viable after many seasons; it is antique clothing combined with what you might make or buy tomorrow, and it is multipurpose clothing that spans a day, a season or a year. This wonderful way of dressing has set a new pace for international design. It is called *American style*.

American style is easy and graceful. It's making your own rules, wearing the clothes that give you comfort and wearing them your way. It's clothing that underscores your collection of beautiful accessories. American style is a positive self-image, an image with confidence, independence, a pride in individual choice and self-indulgence (Illus. 225).

Illus. 225.

148

Find your way back to that confidence of an earlier time. Choose clothing of quality that demonstrates a personal elegance. Opt for the pieces that are fashionable by *your* standards. Show pride in what you wear and how you wear it. When you assemble these clothes, do so on your terms.

Take pleasure in your wardrobe; change the mood freely with your personal collection of accessories. You don't have to chase the latest fads or fancies for your basic garments, but leave the door open for a little indulgence when it comes to your accessories and colors.

Seek a new minimalism, not in the shape of the clothing you choose, but in the amount of clothing you own. Opt for basics that will work in your world—colors and styles that flatter you. Supply yourself with options to your accessory needs.

Accumulate a wardrobe of this type and it will pack in a handbag while it gives you the look of traveling with a department store at your disposal. Keep only those things that fit into the storage space currently available to you; combine them, overlap them, layer them, and accessorize each costume. Your finished look will suggest that you dress from a designer's warehouse.

Being fashionable, well-groomed and well-dressed is a way of life, not a temporary condition (Illus. 226). Work at it. Keep your imagination flowing and your ideas viable. Each of us is unique. Nurture your individuality and make your personal statement.

The end-all of fashion is not a random collection of clothing. It is a personalized wardrobe worn with an attitude of confidence and the joy with which you wear your look. It's the right accessories that turn a single garment into a series of costumes, each with a definitive air. It's the pride of flaunting your own creations, large or small. It's accepting the challenge, exercising your personal flair. But mostly, fashion is enjoying yourself at your ultimate best.

Illus. 226.

METRIC EQUIVALENCY CHART

MM—MILLIMETRES   CM—CENTIMETRES

INCHES TO MILLIMETRES AND CENTIMETRES

INCHES	MM	CM	INCHES	CM	INCHES	CM
⅛	3	0.3	9	22.9	30	76.2
¼	6	0.6	10	25.4	31	78.7
⅜	10	1.0	11	27.9	32	81.3
½	13	1.3	12	30.5	33	83.8
⅝	16	1.6	13	33.0	34	86.4
¾	19	1.9	14	35.6	35	88.9
⅞	22	2.2	15	38.1	36	91.4
1	25	2.5	16	40.6	37	94.0
1¼	32	3.2	17	43.2	38	96.5
1½	38	3.8	18	45.7	39	99.1
1¾	44	4.4	19	48.3	40	101.6
2	51	5.1	20	50.8	41	104.1
2½	64	6.4	21	53.3	42	106.7
3	76	7.6	22	55.9	43	109.2
3½	89	8.9	23	58.4	44	111.8
4	102	10.2	24	61.0	45	114.3
4½	114	11.4	25	63.5	46	116.8
5	127	12.7	26	66.0	47	119.4
6	152	15.2	27	68.6	48	121.9
7	178	17.8	28	71.1	49	124.5
8	203	20.3	29	73.7	50	127.0

YARDS TO METRES

YARDS	METRES	YARDS	METRES	YARDS	METRES	YARDS	METRES	YARDS	METRES
⅛	0.11	2⅛	1.94	4⅛	3.77	6⅛	5.60	8⅛	7.43
¼	0.23	2¼	2.06	4¼	3.89	6¼	5.72	8¼	7.54
⅜	0.34	2⅜	2.17	4⅜	4.00	6⅜	5.83	8⅜	7.66
½	0.46	2½	2.29	4½	4.11	6½	5.94	8½	7.77
⅝	0.57	2⅝	2.40	4⅝	4.23	6⅝	6.06	8⅝	7.89
¾	0.69	2¾	2.51	4¾	4.34	6¾	6.17	8¾	8.00
⅞	0.80	2⅞	2.63	4⅞	4.46	6⅞	6.29	8⅞	8.12
1	0.91	3	2.74	5	4.57	7	6.40	9	8.23
1⅛	1.03	3⅛	2.86	5⅛	4.69	7⅛	6.52	9⅛	8.34
1¼	1.14	3¼	2.97	5¼	4.80	7¼	6.63	9¼	8.46
1⅜	1.26	3⅜	3.09	5⅜	4.91	7⅜	6.74	9⅜	8.57
1½	1.37	3½	3.20	5½	5.03	7½	6.86	9½	8.69
1⅝	1.49	3⅝	3.31	5⅝	5.14	7⅝	6.97	9⅝	8.80
1¾	1.60	3¾	3.43	5¾	5.26	7¾	7.09	9¾	8.92
1⅞	1.71	3⅞	3.54	5⅞	5.37	7⅞	7.20	9⅞	9.03
2	1.83	4	3.66	6	5.49	8	7.32	10	9.14

INDEX

A

accessories
  planning for, 13
  purpose of, 9
  selection of, 15
American style, 148
apron, 47
ascot, 67–68
  neckband, 44
  wearing, 68
Asian women, 19
asymmetric hemline
  circular, peplum with, 98–99
  definition of, 92
  peplum with, 97–98
aviator's scarf, 52, 68–69

B

banded neckline, 45
belting, 82
belts
  with buckles, 81–82
  cabbage rose, 86–88
  double-wrapped, 83–84
  elastic, 88–89
  embroidered, 84–85
  general instructions for, 82–93
  obi-style, 84
  rope, 85–86
  Ultrasuede, 80–81
  wearing, notes on, 75–79
berets, 111–112
  with brim, 115
  darted, 114
  pie-slice large, 115–116
  reversible, 114
  ribbon, 116–119
  unlined, 112–114
Black women, 19

blondes, 19–20
  deep, 21
  pale, 20–21
bows, hair, 122–123
bracelet cuff, 36–37
brunettes, 24–25
bubble hemline, 92
buckles, styles of, 81–82

C

cabbage rose, 124–125
  belt, 86–88
  hat, 121
closet, contents of, 11–12
clothing, wearable, 11
cocktail hats, 119–123
collars
  for dickeys, 32–33, 35–36, 37
  leaf, 131–133
  measurements for, 33
  for transformation dickey, 43
colors, *see also* personal color analysis
  genetic, 9
  personal, information on, 9
color samples, 17, 25–26
cuffs, 36–37
  bracelet, 36–37

D

darted waistline, 94–95
dickeys, 26, 27
  basic pattern for, 30–33
  button-front, 35
  collars for, 35–36, 37
  definition of, 29–30
  from knitted fabric, 40–41
  measurements for basic pattern, 33–35
  pleated, 39–40
  with pleated neckband, 38–39

ruffled, 37–38
transformation, 41–45

E
elastic belts, 88–89
embroidered belts, 84–85
eyes, 17

F
fabric
   found, 13
   for overskirts, 91
figure type, belts for, 75–79
fishnet triangle scarf, 64
flamenco-style overskirt, 102–104
flounce, 91
flowers, fabric
   cabbage rose, 124–125
   lazy daisies, 128–130
   small rose, 125–127
fringe, hand-tied, 68–69

G
glitter, decorations with, 134–137

H
hair color, 18–19
   blonde, 19–21
   brunette, 24–25
   red, 22–23
hats
   beret, 111–119
   cocktail, 119–123
hemlines, for overskirts, 91–92

I
interlocking buckle, 82

J
jabot, 54
   lettuce edge ruffled, 65–66
jeweled motifs, 136
jewelry, 26–27
jewels, large, 137

K
knitted fabric, dickeys of, 40–41

L
lace, 91

leaf collar, 131–133
lettuce edge ruffled jabot, 65–66

M
measurements, for collars, 33
motifs, jeweled or sequined, 136

N
nail polish, 26
neckband, ascot, 44

O
obi-style belt, 84
overskirts
   fabric for, 91
   flamenco-style, 102–104
   general information, 91–92
   hemlines for, 91–92
   length of, 91
   longer-length, 99
   tiered, 101
   usefulness of, 90
   waistline for, 92–95

P
padded head scarf, 62
paint sticks, 137
peplum
   with asymmetric hemline, 97–98
   circle-cut, 96–97
   circular asymmetric, 98–99
   fabric for, 91
   pocket, 105–109
   straight-cut, 95–96
personal color analysis, 16
   brunette, 24–25
   color samples for, 17, 25–26
   equipment for, 16–17
   eyes and, 17
   hair and, 18–19
   redhead, 22–23
   skin tone and, 19
   using your colors, 26–28
pleated dickey, 39–40
pleated neckband, for dickey, 38–39
pocket peplum, 105–109

Q
quilted jewelry, 138–139
   general directions, 139–146
   inspiration and source material for, 139

R

redheads, 22–23
rhinestones, 137
ribbons, hair, 122–123
rope belts, 85–86
rose, small fabric, 125–127

S

scarves
  aviator's, 52, 68–69
  fishnet triangle, 64
  hems and finishes for, 55–56
  knotting of, 70–71
  large squares, 58–61
  padded head, 62
  rectangular, 52–53, 66–74
  round, 54
  square, 48–51
  theatre, 68
  triangular, 54–55
  turban, 63–64
  usefulness of, 26, 27, 46–47
  wearing, notes on, 56–58
seasonal wardrobe, 13–14
sequins, 135–136
shoe paint, 27

skin tone, 19
stardust, 137
strings, sequin, 136

T

theatre scarf, 68
tiered overskirts, 101
transformation dickey, 41–45
turbans, 63–64

U

Ultrasuede belts, 80–81

V

visor variation, 121–122

W

waistband, *see also under specific project*
waistline, for overskirts, 92–95
wardrobe
  current, assessment of, 12–13
  definition of, 9, 10
  planning, 12
  seasonal, 13–14
  workable, 12, 150

ABOUT THE AUTHOR

Rusty Bensussen's many talents have made her an entry in *Who's Who in American Women.* As a fine artist, her paintings have been exhibited in New York, San Francisco, Seattle and Portland in the U.S., Vancouver, B.C., in Canada. A best-selling author of sewing books, her works are known throughout the English-speaking world. Current books in print are: *Making Patterns from Finished Clothes; Making a Complete Wardrobe from 4 Basic Patterns; Shortcuts to a Perfect Sewing Pattern.*

A strong interest in high-style clothing led her to the Chicago Academy of Fine Arts, where she studied fashion design and illustration. She later worked as a fashion illustrator and copy writer at Marshall Field and Company, The Fair Store, The Boston Store, and Carson Pirie Scott and Company, all in Chicago. She has written sewing articles for *Sew News* and is currently a contributor to *Sew-It-Seams Magazine.*

A two-week vacation on the West Coast was the start of a serious love affair with Seattle, Washington, where she still makes her home.

She has taught sewing and other fashion-related classes and seminars at Broadway/Edison J.C. and was on staff for several fabric shops in the greater Seattle area.

She is a wife, mother of two married daughters, grandmother of five grandchildren. Relaxing, in her vocabulary, means never sitting down with empty hands. She writes about sewing, illustrates her books and articles, designs most of her personal wardrobe, does her own sewing, puts on seminars, makes bobbin lace, knits, crochets, paints, and travels with her husband, who recently retired.